HOW HELL DO WE MOTIVATE THESE KIDS?

TODD STANLEY

FIRST
Educational Resources

POWERFUL • AFFORDABLE • SUSTAINABLE

Published by:
FIRST Educational Resources, LLC
Winneconne, Wisconsin
www.firsteducation-us.com
info@firsteducation-us.com
ISBN: 978-1-7332390-5-9

Printed in the United States of America
(EnvisionInk Printing Solutions, Neenah, WI)

About the Author

Todd Stanley is a National Board teacher and the author of many teacher-education books including *Project-Based Learning for Gifted Students: A Handbook for the 21st Century Classroom (2nd edition), When Smart Kids Underachieve in the Classroom: Practical Solutions for Teachers, Authentic Learning: Real World Experiences that Build 21st Century Skills,* and his latest, *Promoting Rigor Through Higher-Level Questioning.* He served as a classroom teacher for 18 years where he taught 2nd graders thru seniors in high school. He is currently the gifted services coordinator for Pickerington Local Schools in central Ohio where he lives with his wife Nicki and two daughters, Anna and Abby. You can follow him on Twitter @the_gifted_guy or visit his website at thegiftedguy.com where you can access blogs, resources, and view presentations he has given.

Table of Contents

Dedication

This book is dedicated to Steve Shapiro, my cooperative teacher during my student teaching. He taught me three important things:

1. There are many other experiences that educate our students other than what happens within the four walls of the class-room.

2. Student voice is very important, so make sure to do more listening than talking.

3. If you don't like what you are doing, change it.

He also showed me how effective all-inclusive project-based learning can be. Steve has remained a friend and mentor through my over 20 years of teaching, and I often wake up in the middle of the night in a cold sweat thinking about how my educational career might have been different, had I not been fortunate enough to have been paired with him. Everyone should be so lucky to have a Steve Shapiro to bounce ideas off and to be challenged by.

I also want to thank the thousands of students I have had over the years who have influenced and shaped me to be the teacher I am. Without your voice, I would not have been able to write this book.

Introduction

THE GAME OF SCHOOL

"Education is what remains after one
has forgotten what one has learned at school."
- Albert Einstein

How Much Have Schools Really Changed?

I was having a conversation with an educator during her final year in the classroom, and she was commenting on how much teaching had changed over the course of her career. I thought about it for a minute and asked her, "How has it changed?" Her response was the easy, go-to change that general society has gone through in the last couple of decades: the breakneck pace of new technology. Now, instead of blackboards, we have SMARTboards; instead of overheads, we have LCD projectors; instead of going to the library or getting a set of encyclopedias, students can access the Internet at their fingertips. These are indeed changes to the classroom, but are they really changes to teaching? Each of those new pieces of technology basically does the same thing that their predecessor did before them. It might be faster, or easier to manipulate, or cooler, but it is the same basic premise.

I have been in education for over 20 years. In that time, I have seen lots of changes come along: outcomes-based education, the inclusion movement, small schools, STEM, and a host of others. When you wipe away the veneer from these shiny new initiatives, however, you are left with the same elements of school there have always been: the bell rings, kids move to a subject-specific classroom together with others their age, the bell rings again, they go to another. In each of these classes, students are taught material that has been laid out for them. Then, they must show mastery of said material through some kind of assessment. This usually comes in the form of a grade. If a student receives an A, it indicates that she is doing very well, a C shows that she is having some struggles, and an F means that something is seriously amiss.

This is how school was when my parents went; it is the same as when I attended; it is the way it is now that my children are going to school. If we are not careful, it is how it will be for the next generation of children. The question is, why hasn't teaching changed that much? This is the fundamental problem in education: most people, from parents to teachers to politicians, want our current crop of kids to have the same education they had when they were in school. I cannot tell you how many parents have come in lamenting that we were no longer teaching cursive writing, or that they want math to be taught the way it was when they were in school, with direct instruction and worksheets. This always amazes me considering how people need to have the most up-to-date cell phone that is available, while promoting traditional, outdated forms of education. The educational equivalent to the traditional phone would involve one with a hand crank to connect your call through the operator and speak into the receiver. Is that really the education we want for our children?

Now it is a Game

Like anything that doesn't change frequently, people have learned how to play the game of school. There are certain hoops that we expect students to jump through, such as attending class, turning in assignments, taking tests, and following directions. Like most games, those who are compliant and follow the rules tend to be more successful. Unfortunately, for those who choose *not* to play the game, whether because of disillusionment, lack of resources, or inability, school is more difficult. Moreover, because these students are not playing the game, there is no system in place to help them. After all, you have to play the game in order to have access to this system.

All games have rules. Some of these are written in the rule book, but some unspoken rules are just as powerful. For instance, consider the game of baseball. There is a thick rule book for the sport, and yet there are so many unwritten rules. Here are some of them:

- Don't step in front of the catcher on the way to the batter's box.
- Don't steal a base if your team is up by a lot of runs.
- Don't admire a home run or flip your bat.
- Don't try to break up a no-hitter with a bunt.
- No one but the pitcher should step on the pitcher's mound.

What happens if you break any of these unwritten rules? There are no penalties or score losses that officials would administer. Instead, the baseball players police themselves, and a rule-breaker is more than likely to get a fastball in their ribs the next time they step to the plate.

School has unwritten rules as well. Although breaking them will not result in a baseball to the ribs, it will hurt your chances of doing well. Here are some of the unwritten rules in school:

- Compliant kids get better grades than those who are not.
- If you try, a teacher is going to find a way to pass you.
- Hard work takes you a lot further than ability.
- There are students who take advanced classes and AP courses, and then there are 'those' kids.
- Teachers do have favorites.

Probably the most prevalent unwritten rule of school is that grades are used as a carrot. In this metaphor, farmers motivate a donkey to do what they want by tying a carrot to a string, which is then attached to a stick. The farmer holds the stick out, keeping the carrot right in front of the donkey's line of sight, but just out of reach. This motivates the animal to move forward in order to reach the carrot.

Schools do the exact same thing with students. They use grades as the carrot, assuming that by dangling the promise of good ones, it will entice everyone to move forward. The problem is that this technique does not work for every student. Some kids are not motivated by or attracted to grades. In fact, because they are unwilling to play the game of school, they place very little value on grades. This, then, becomes a perpetual cycle; in order to try and get them to improve, teachers use grades as a motivator. Worse yet, schools believe the threat of bad grades will motivate these students. You can see the problem with this: If you are a student who doesn't care about grades, why are grades, even bad ones, going to make you care or motivate you? There is nothing to entice you to learn.

The narrative we sell to children at a very young age is if you get good grades, you will do well in school; in turn, if you do well in school, you will have a better chance at a good life. Like the belief in Santa Claus, some kids buy into this hook, line, and sinker, while others— for various reasons—remain skeptical, if not complete non-believers. And just like Santa Claus, the older children get, the more they begin to question the myth presented to them. There are some kids who for whatever reason, don't believe in the value of grades or care about what they get. The big question becomes, how can you find what will motivate them? How do you make schools in which students are learning for the sake of learning, not for a perceived reward?

Studies have shown the detrimental effects of using grades to motivate students:

- Grades tend to diminish students' interest in whatever they're learning (Kohn, 2018).
- Grades promote a fear of failure, even in high-achieving students (Pulfrey et al., 2011).

- Grades create a preference for the easiest possible task (Kage, 1991).

- Grades are associated with increased levels of cheating (Anderman & Murdock, 2007).

- Grades tend to reduce the quality of students' thinking (Kohn, 2018).

In Alfie Kohn's book *Punished by Rewards: The Trouble with Gold Stars, Incentive Plans, A's, Praise, and Other Bribes*, the conclusions were drawn from a review of hundreds of studies. The results demonstrated people actually do lower-quality work when enticed with grades. Kohn's central argument was that the use of rewards such as grades to change people's behavior is not effective long-term.

This book proposes that if truly no child is going to be left behind and if it is indeed possible for every student to succeed, educators need to do a better job of not using carrots to motivate students. As for what should be used instead...How about their love of learning? This is not a novel idea, but this focus shifts the motivation from extrinsic to intrinsic. It is necessary to discard the assumption that all students are motivated by just grades; instead, educators find out what truly motivates each one of them and use that as the enticing motivator to get buy-in for learning. Of course, there are a lot of questions, such as: How do I do that? What does that look like in the classroom? and What do I need to change in my teaching practices? In this book, I will answer all of these questions and more.

The first of these questions is the WHY. Why do we need to find a different way? What proof do we have that grades are not working as the sole motivator for students in our schools? What can we point to in order to show that maybe it is not working in its current form? And why must things change?

When you look at the reasons students drop out of high school, the top two identified by America's Promise Alliance were (a) failing too many classes and (b) because they were bored (Gould, 2015).

Figure 0.1 *Top Reasons Students Drop Out of High School*

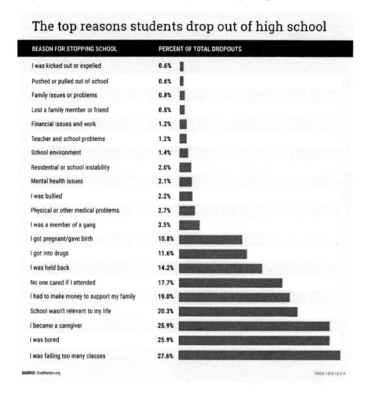

The top reasons students drop out of high school

REASON FOR STOPPING SCHOOL	PERCENT OF TOTAL DROPOUTS
I was kicked out or expelled	0.6%
Pushed or pulled out of school	0.6%
Family issues or problems	0.8%
Lost a family member or friend	0.8%
Financial issues and work	1.2%
Teacher and school problems	1.2%
School environment	1.4%
Residential or school instability	2.0%
Mental health issues	2.1%
I was bullied	2.2%
Physical or other medical problems	2.7%
I was a member of a gang	3.5%
I got pregnant/gave birth	10.8%
I got into drugs	11.6%
I was held back	14.2%
No one cared if I attended	17.7%
I had to make money to support my family	19.0%
School wasn't relevant to my life	20.3%
I became a caregiver	25.9%
I was bored	25.9%
I was failing too many classes	27.6%

SOURCE: GradNation.org   TECH INSIDER

Instead of leaving school as a result of getting into drugs, having an unstable home life, needing to support family, or other external factors, many kids are dropping out because of school factors. Let's take the 27% who are failing too many classes. We need to dig a little deeper into that. What are the causes of the failing grade? Is it because the student is not capable of doing the work, or is it that he is not willing to do it? Compliance is a very large part of navigating through high school. As I've already mentioned, playing the game of school makes things so much easier than not playing it. How many of these students who were failing too many classes were simply not willing to play the game of school? How many of them had the ability to pass the class, but the grade wasn't a good enough motivator? More importantly, if those students had been motivated in another way, would they not have failed the class?

Second, 25.9% dropped out because they were bored. That means that one quarter of all dropouts do so because school is not engaging enough to make them want to stick around, not because of a lack of ability. This engagement versus ability is very much a factor when considering that of those who drop out of high school, nearly 25% of them are identified as gifted in one area or more (Center, 2008). This means that gifted students—the ones with the most potential—are not graduating. The question is, if it is not ability that is preventing them from completing school, what is?

Many theorists have tried to explain this. Busteed (2013) contended, "Ranging from our overzealous focus on standardized testing and curricula to our lack of experiential and project-based learning pathways for students—not to mention the lack of pathways for students who will not and do not want to go on to college" (para. 6). This is the problem with playing the game of school; most schools are set up for a certain type of student learning a certain way. This leaves out those who do not fit this model. There really isn't anywhere for 'those students' to go, except down the path of failure and possible dropout. As the esteemed Taylor Swift said, "You play stupid games, you win stupid prizes."

The reality is that no matter what pathways are created for students, we need to figure out ways to motivate every kid. If grades are not a big enough motivator, we need to do something else. Also telling is the fact that 20.3% of students stated that school wasn't relevant to their lives. It is necessary to connect learning to their lives as well. We need to find another way.

The next of these questions is the HOW. Instead of using the extrinsic factors of grades or other such rewards to motivate students, how do we motivate them intrinsically by tapping into their innate curiosity? There is a formula that teachers can follow in order to create lessons and classroom environments that allow children to find and pursue their love of learning. There are six phases to creating this culture of motivation:

1. **Caring:** This involves getting to know your students, their interests, and the context of their learning.

2. **Visible learning:** This requires focusing lessons that allow students to clearly understand what they are learning, and more importantly, why they are doing so.

3. **Student choice/autonomy:** This phase includes giving students as many choices as possible in the *what, how, when,* and *where* of their learning. This makes them a partner in their own learning.

4. **Authentic learning:** Having a classroom that is engaging and authentic will show students the lesson's place in context to the real-world, as well as the relevance to their own lives.

5. **Effective management:** Educators must manage their classroom optimally in order to support and guide students so they are all able to follow their love of learning. This will look very different from a traditional classroom.

6. **Reflection:** This phase involves providing space and guidance to facilitate purposeful reflection to determine the learning that students actually did, not the learning intended for them.

This culture of motivation is all about creating life-long learners by providing them with the opportunity to learn relevant skills that will lead to a greater chance at success in the real world. It does this by making students care about what they are learning so they are more apt to learn it, and it teaches them many 21st century skills through authentic learning. Some of the skills they will learn will be:

- Collaboration and teamwork
- Creativity and imagination
- Critical thinking
- Problem-solving
- Oral and written communication skills

- Social responsibility and citizenship
- Technology literacy
- Initiative/drive

How will learning these skills prepare students for the real world? Because they are relevant to what employers are looking for in the job market (Worthington, 2014).

Figure 0.2 *Skills Companies Demand in New Hires*

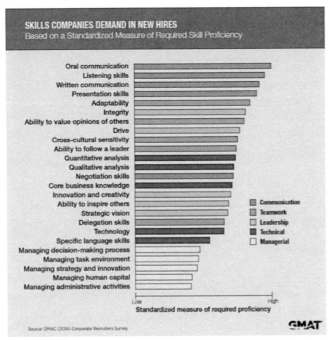

As you can see, it is these 21st century 'soft skills' that are more desired by the corporate world. Knowledge of business is of medium importance according to this survey, while oral communication, adaptability, and drive are all above this. If you want to do your students a favor and provide them with relevant skills that will be useful for them in their occupation and will lead to professional success, look no further than this list.

The authentic strategies provided in your culture of motivation will enable you to teach the required content standards, while at the same time allowing students to learn these 21st century skills. This, of course, is easier said than done. After all, you can lead a horse to water, but he may not choose to drink. The question for those students who are unwilling to play this game of school is, how the hell do we motivate them?

Chapter 1

HOW THE HELL DO WE MOTIVATE THESE KIDS?

"Our greatest fear should not be of failure, but of succeeding at things in life that don't really matter."
- Francis Chan

That is the million-dollar question: How do you motivate kids who don't seem to be motivated? What program do we use? What curriculum would be best? What strategy do we employ? Like most things in life, there is no one single answer. This is why grades don't act as a motivator for all kids. We have to consider everything that will motivate a child, because what works for one may not for another.

Part of this is the personalization of their learning. If you are not making it personal, they are going to have a difficult time seeing the relevance of what they are learning. Without relevance, their motivation begins to wane, and this leads to kids not caring about what they are learning. As cognitive scientist Dan Willingham stated, "We remember better those things that are meaningful to us" (Willingham, 2009, p. 44). This premise seems simple enough. If teachers are not making it relevant for each student, this is hurting the chances of a child to remember what he is learning.

What Causes Kids to Lose Motivation?

I have been teaching for over 20 years, and have been a parent nearly just as long, so I have seen this from both sides. I have taught third graders all the way to seniors in high school, so I can tell you without compunction that children are way more motivated learners when they are younger. Trying to get a second grader to learn about what makes a flower grow is easy as can be. That second grader is curious as to just what does make a flower grow, so she is much more likely to get on board and interested in what is being taught. If you ask a senior in high school to learn about what makes plants grow in an environmental science class, it is going to be more of a challenge because she is going to have difficulty determining when she would ever need such knowledge unless she were going to become a botanist. If you don't believe me, just look at this Gallup data on school engagement (Busteed, 2013):

Figure 1.1 *The School Cliff*

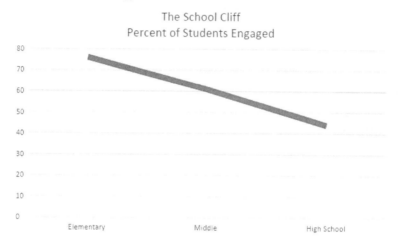

In elementary school, three out of every four (75%) kids feel engaged in their learning. This begins to drop off in middle school, falling to 60%, until high school, where less than half feel engaged. Experts have termed this 'the school cliff.' Let me give you a real-life example.

My Daughters

I have experienced this school cliff with my daughters. When my older daughter went to her first day of school in the first grade, this is how excited she was.

Notice that she is wearing a grin from ear to ear, her cheekbones are high, her shoulders are raised in anticipation, and she is wearing her best dress. During this time period, she loved to go to school, being disappointed when the weekend came or was told she had a day off. And why wouldn't she love it? She was learning so many new things, things that she found shiny and interesting. She carried this smile to school nearly every day, and when I asked her how her day was, she shared stories of what she learned, whether it was why bears hibernate to what makes a light bulb work. I always enjoyed our nearly 30-minute car ride home from school, turning off the radio and listening to the tunes of what new things she had learned that day.

As the years went by, I noticed a slight waning in her enthusiasm concerning school. Here is the photo of her first day of school for sixth grade. You will see a few differences from the first-grade picture. Notice that the wide grin is still there, although the cheekbones are not as high. Her shoulders are not as poised in anticipation of the coming school year, and her outfit—although a very stylish one—does not give off the same excitement as wearing one's best dress. This lessening of excitement about school manifested itself in other ways too. She was eager when the weekend came, always grumbling a little when Sunday evening rolled around, and she had to get prepared for school the next day.

Her enthusiasm to tell me about her day had also been reduced to a *Reader's Digest Condensed* version. I felt fortunate on those days when

I got a sentence out of her; even then, many times, it had to be goaded out of her. I think she would admit to liking school, but the love affair was over. School was beginning to become something she had to do, rather than something she wanted to do. When she came home, she was quick to move through her homework so that she could pursue other things that she loved learning more, such as designing jewelry or playing tennis.

By the time she got to her final year of school, she had become one of the disengaged. In this photo on the first day of her senior year, the smile is still there, but the cheekbones are low. This was because the smile was not a result of her being genuinely happy to be going to school, but because I asked her to for the picture. The second the photo was taken, her smile disappeared. You may also see her slumped shoulders and her more casual get-up, complete with sandals.

High school for her had become a weigh station where she was biding time until she could go to college—where she would learn what she was really interested in. It was at this point that I had stopped asking her what she did that day at school because I got tired at the one-word grunts of "fine" or shrugged shoulders. Keep in mind, my daughter was not a poor student. Much to the contrary, she graduated with a 4.1 grade point average, but imagine those students who were not willing to play this game of school and let their disengagement affect their grades.

I thought maybe this was just my oldest daughter. After all, she had pretty much been born a cynic, so it would be easy for school to become tiresome for her. A much better litmus test would be my youngest daughter. She liked everything, and had difficulty saying when she did not because she didn't want anyone to get their feelings hurt. Surely, I would not see this cliff with her.

 Here she is on her first day of fourth grade (told you). Her smile is so wide that it caused her eyes to squint, and she gave the double thumbs up for good measure. This was her attitude throughout the school year. She loved her teachers, her classes, and school. She had not a harsh word to say about it, and never seemed to have a bad day. When I asked her about her day, she would fill the entire 15-minute walk home with tales of the wonderful things she had learned. We sometimes had to take another loop around the block in order for her to share everything. She was always disappointed when the weekend came around, and couldn't wait to get back to school. She even cried when school let out for summer. I knew I would not see the cliff with her.

 As with most things concerning my daughters, I was wrong. This shirt sums up quite nicely how she came to feel about school. Although she still liked her teachers, her classes, and school, there were definite signs that the love was beginning to wane. When it would start snowing in the evening, her first thoughts turned to hoping for a day off. Weekends became sought-after, and she counted down the days until summer break. Even during the 2 months that she didn't physically go to school because of COVID-19, she did not miss school; rather, she missed her friends who went to school with her.

The Power of Student Choice

The final piece of evidence that convinced me that middle and high school were the place where the love of learning went to die came on my older daughter's first day of college. When her mother and I called her, I asked that fateful question of how her day was. She proceeded to talk for over an hour about how great her classes were, how she was learning so much, and more importantly, she couldn't wait until the next day so she could learn even more. That love of learning that I hadn't seen for a few years was back. What was the difference?

When I reflected on this, two things came into play to reignite this love of learning. First was that she took enough AP and College Credit Plus classes in high school so that she did not have to take those boring weed-out classes that most universities throw at incoming freshmen. All of the classes she was taking directly tied in with the major she had chosen, meaning that she was interested in them. The second was that my daughter had the good sense to pursue a major that she felt spoke to her strengths and interests; thus, she was excited about anything having to do with it. She could definitely see the relevance of what she was learning and how she would use this later in her career. She didn't sit in any classes wondering, "Why am I having to learn this? This is something I will never need for the rest of my life." Instead, she considered what part of the puzzle this particular class was and it fit into her long-term plans.

The major difference between high school and college was that she had *chosen* her major at the university, meaning she had decided the path that her learning would take. It was this power of choice that made such a big difference in her motivation. In primary and secondary school, how often are students given choice? Some would argue at the high school level you have choices in the classes one takes, but I would argue that a pathway had been established long before that, and students had options rather than choices. A kid in high school can't say, "I'm not interested in math, so I'm not taking any more math classes." There are still the core classes that must be taken due to graduation requirements.

The modern school system has a Renaissance Man mentality, where everyone has to be mediocre at everything, rather than focusing on strengths and interests and becoming really good at them. Imagine that in your sophomore year in high school, you decided that English/Language Arts was your strong suit and got you jazzed up, so you took three ELA classes and skipped the math and science courses. A high school would never let you do this, but this is exactly what I got to do when I went to college. I declared myself a Creative Writing major, took a majority of writing or literature classes, and did not have to take one single dreaded math class in college. What effect did this have on my motivation? My high school GPA was a 2.50, while in college it was a 3.60; in graduate school, where I got into something that I was even more motivated about, it became a 3.90. Having a choice certainly had a major impact on my motivation, and my grades got better as a result. I will discuss this phenomenon further in Chapter Five.

Different Types of Motivation

According to psychologists, intrinsic motivation is the best and most effective type of motivation. This means not doing something because you are told to, but because you want to. For example, a student is studying for a test. There are two ways this can be approached. One of the typical manners is where students are afraid of getting a bad grade, so they study to avoid this. What they end up doing is cramming, which is learning it just long enough to take the test. On the other hand, studying is intrinsically motivated, meaning that students are curious about something and want to learn more so they study about it. This could be coming across a musician they like and listening to some of his catalog, or wanting to learn how to crochet so they watch videos showing how. Anyone who is really good at something does not cram—they study, whether it be a chess master, a tennis player, or a teacher. What if, instead, a student studied because he was genuinely interested in learning about something, because his curiosity led him there? Wouldn't that be revolutionary?

Isn't that what kids do all of the time when they go on YouTube to learn how to play a video game or how to properly apply makeup, when they search the Internet far and wide to learning how to do a DIY project, or when they learn how to ride a skateboard by watching others? How many times does that skateboarder attempt a grind, failing over and over, until he finally achieves success? Because he is curious, he is motivated to persist, however many times it takes. What if—and this is a big if—schools were the places that students went to satiate this curiosity?

As teachers, we need to find ways to trigger this intrinsic motivation in our students. You might not be able to get a student excited about decimals or the Mesopotamians, but you can provide them with a product that makes them curious, such as creating a website or building a clay replica. There are ways to get students excited about topics when the topics aren't very exciting.

Goal Valuation

If you are going to personalize student motivation, you must be familiar with its three component factors. These three components are collectively known as *goal valuation*:

Figure 1.2 *Three Factors of Student Motivation*

How **_interesting_** does the student find what is being taught? Is it something that intrigues or excites him, or does it do the opposite and bore him?

How **_important_** does the student consider what is being taught? It is something he believes he is going to use later in life or what sort of relevance does it have for him now?

How **_attainable_** is completion the task or having success with this work? If the student can see how to accomplish this task, he will be more willing to give it a try. If he thinks there is no way he is going to be able to get through this, the question becomes why even bother?

Keep in mind, as educators, we cannot make students find something interesting, important, or attainable. We can certainly suggest it, but students must decide for themselves how much value they are going to put toward each of these goals. There are factors that teachers can control. We can make an assignment seem more interesting by presenting it in an engaging way. Or, if we want students to see the importance of a lesson, we can try and show them how it will be used in the real world. We also can make the expectations crystal clear to students so that they can see what is needed for success. What we cannot control, however, is whether students find value in these. No matter how engaging we make the lesson, how important we show it to be, or how clear we make it, there are still going to be some students who do not see the value in one, two, or even all of these.

Students fall into three different types. Type A only needs one of these factors to be present in order to be motivated. For example, if a teacher is giving a lesson on fractions and in the introduction, shows students how fractions are used to determine statistics for baseball, a student who likes baseball might find this interesting and thus be motivated. He may not understand why learning fractions is important or how to attain mastery, but that does not matter; the interest has him hooked.

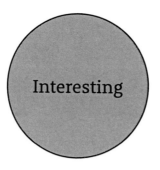

Another Type A student is in a class in which she is learning the state capitals. The teacher is using drill and kill to memorize the names of the cities and connecting them to the state—not the most exciting method. Despite this, the student believes that this is important to learn because her father travels a lot for his work. She sees how this knowledge could be important in the real world, so she is on board for learning it, regardless of how tedious a method is used.

Type B students need to see the value in two of these factors in order to be motivated. If one is there, but the other is not, it will be difficult for them to become engaged. An example would be a student whose teacher has done a pretty good job convincing him what is interesting about reading the novel *War and Peace*, but the kid takes one look at the thickness of the book and has difficulty seeing how he is going to get through this in his lifetime, much less a school year. It does not seem attainable, so even though the interest to read it is there, the ability to see how this can be done is not. He does not need to understand why reading the book would be important, but does need to find it both interesting and attainable.

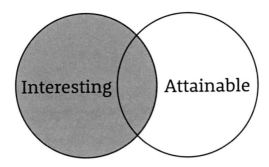

Another Type B student works hard for his Spanish teacher because she is really funny and makes the class interesting. In addition, she makes connections for how the learning will be used in the future, so he also sees the importance. It does not matter that in the Spanish class the year before, he was barely able to maintain a C average. Even though foreign language is not his best subject, this teacher has managed to make it both important and interesting, resulting in the student's motivation.

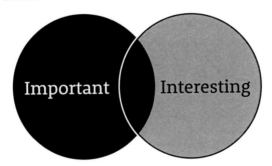

The toughest nut to crack is the Type C student, who has to see all three of these in order to be motivated. If any one of them is missing, the motivation of this student takes a dive. A student is doing well on a unit concerning physical versus chemical change because the teacher has made the student see the relevance to his life, she has shown him clearly how to manage his time so completing the unit seems doable, and he thinks it is a pretty interesting topic.

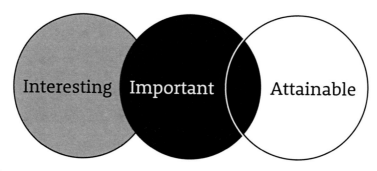

When the class moves on to electricity, the same student has trouble turning in his work and is not as successful as the previous unit. The teacher has done everything she did before, showing the relevance of knowing how electricity works and giving a rubric at the beginning of the unit to show how to attain mastery, but the student just does not find electricity that interesting. Because he is a Type C student and he has not placed much value on its interest, he is not going to give the same effort he did when he saw the value of all three.

For further explanation, watch a video tutorial at
https://youtu.be/-EusDip1EkA.

Why Do We Want Them Motivated, Not Just Compliant?

Just being compliant causes students to have a fear of failing. Because the grade is the motivator, those who are compliant play it safe. They don't want to take any risks that might affect their grade, so instead of swinging big and producing something truly amazing that would demonstrate their love of learning, they do what they think the teachers and schools want. This does not sound very motivating to me. If you don't believe me, Jessica Lahey (2016) expressed this so much better in her book *The Gift of Failure*:

> The Truth—for this parent and so many others—is this: Marianna has sacrificed her natural curiosity and love of learning at the altar of achievement, and it's our fault. Her parent, her teachers, society at large-we are all implicated in this crime against learning. From her first day of school, we

pointed her toward that altar and trained her to measure her progress toward that goal by means of points, scores, and awards...Above all else, we taught her to fear failure, and that fear has destroyed her love of learning.

As teachers, we reassure students that it's OK to fail, and then turn around and grade their homework or take off points because they made a small mistake, even though they understood the general idea. If it really is OK to fail, we must create classrooms where there is space for kids to take risks. After all, when we take risks, that is where the learning takes place. The figure below illustrates the different levels of learning:

Figure 1.3 *Levels of Learning*

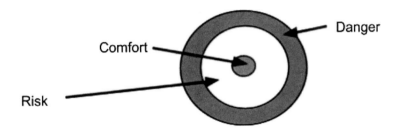

In the center is the comfort zone. Here, learners are covering material they possibly already know or that comes to them easily; although it feels safe, there is not much learning taking place. On the outer edge of learning is the danger zone. If you push students too hard, too fast, and/or with materials that are too unfamiliar, they might become fearful and shut down, meaning little to no learning is taking place there either. Students in this zone do not see how to attain success, so they simply don't try. Why take a big risk, if you fear that there is too much danger of being punished with a poor grade? For the most effective learning environment, students must walk the precarious tightrope of the risk zone. They must be challenged, feeling a little out of their comfort zone, but not so much that they fear failure. That is the optimal place for learning to take place. That is where the love of learning will be discovered.

It is a difficult task for teachers to maintain this balancing act, so not a lot of teachers do so. We know this because the risk zone is where engagement takes place, and yet students are reporting they are not engaged. We need to find ways to get students in the risk zone without frightening them off.

Finding the Heart of It

In order to motivate students, we must recognize which of these values are important to each of them and make sure we do our best to address them. This still does not guarantee complete success for your students. In the next part of the book, I will provide you with strategies for addressing all three of these values. How can you do this? By finding ways to tap into their interests and passions where they are intrinsically motivated.

How do we get kids to love learning? It's not like we have to instill or program this love of learning into them. Children are born with this. From the moment they come into this world, they are curious about it and the goings-on around them. They want to touch everything, they want to explore everywhere, they want to ask a billion questions. They are literally itching to learn.

Instead, what we should be doing is figuring out ways to avoid blocking this love of learning. The way schools are currently set up, however, this is what tends to happen. We can start by finding a better way to help students see the interest, importance, and attainability in everything they are learning.

Chapter 2

CREATING A CULTURE OF MOTIVATION

"Motivation is what gets you started.
Habit is what keeps you going."
- Jim Ryun

That still leaves us with the question of HOW you motivate these kids, especially if what motivates each of them is different. The answer is fairly simple: there is no one answer. The grade as the motivator has been the one answer for a long time, and we have already established that this is not working. Just replacing it with another extrinsic reward would not solve the problem; it would just make a different problem. Like most things in life, the answer is multi-layered, in that there is no single answer for all students. You will need to come up with answers for each of them.

The Basics

The best way to achieve goal valuation is to provide personalized learning that drills down to what motivates each of your students. Just like the quote at the start of this chapter, motivation is the beginning of the learning process. Once you have them motivated, you can teach your students habits that will allow them to be successful, as well as the content standards for which you are responsible. In order to do this, you must create a culture of motivation in your classroom that allows students to be intrinsically driven. The phases to creating this are:

- Caring
- Visible Learning
- Student Choice
- Authentic Learning
- Effective Management
- Reflection

I would characterize these as phases, rather than steps. Steps denote that you must go in a particular order to achieve the goal in mind. For instance, recipes have steps. If you go out of order, the results can be a bad meal. You can change the order of phases, though. You might put your "reflection" phase at the middle of your lesson, rather than waiting until the end. Or, you might start with student choice in the beginning, instead of introducing the lesson first. Steps also give the idea of having to finish one before you begin the next. These phases overlap with one another, and you might find yourself in a number of them at the same time. Phases such as effective management and caring are things you are doing all the time, rather than at specific moments, but it is all of these phases meshed together that leads to student engagement. You can certainly engage students without doing all of them but by having all of these phases of motivation, you are getting more fish in the net so to speak. Because different students are motivated by different things, having multiple strategies that induce motivation means you are going to reach more students. You are truly leaving no child behind.

The rest of this chapter will be a brief description of what each of these phases looks like—a snapshot, so to speak, until we get into the more detailed chapters, which provide specific strategies that you can use in the classroom to help deliver each of them.

Caring

This phase is relatively simple in concept, but more complex in execution. It simply involves showing your students you care, both about them and about the class you are teaching. This can come in various forms, but ultimately, if your students don't think *you* care, it is going to be difficult for *them* to care.

The question then becomes, how do you show students that you care? This does not mean being touchy/feely with your emotions, becoming their friend, or being a hugger. I was never that sort of teacher, but I'm pretty sure most of my students felt as though I cared about them as people and that I cared about what I was teaching. Why am I pretty sure? Because students who haven't been in my classroom for 25 years still reach out to me through social media. I have lunch with students I had in the seventh grade and are now adults. And I constantly run into parents who tell me about the impact I had on their children.

I'll never forget a student I had my second year of teaching who was a curious sort. I had this brochure on my desk that I had picked up at some conference labeled "101 things you can do to show students you care." I saw him looking it over. He then turned to me and said, "Mr. Stanley, you don't do any of these things."

I'd be lying if I said that didn't sting a little. A list of 101 ways to show you care, and he didn't think I did any of them. I had some work to do.

I decided the best way to show I cared was to form relationships with my students. There are a couple of schools of thought on the relationship between a teacher and a student. One end of the spectrum has teachers putting up a barrier and keeping it strictly professional, not getting to know students personally. The rationale behind this attitude is that teaching is a job, and the job is to teach kids, not to be their best bud. The other end of the spectrum is the teacher who wants to be best friends with all of the students. This is usually a very popular teacher, but there isn't always a high level of respect. Like most things in life, the most ideal place to be is somewhere in the middle where there is a clear distinction between the adult and the child, while at the same time allowing space to get to know one another. This is where I decided I needed to be.

I had a distinct advantage in that we looped students, meaning I had kids for 2 years, which gave me plenty of time to get to know them and show I cared. How did I show this? When it came to showing my students that I cared about them, there were three things that helped convey this:

1. Asking

2. Listening

3. Sharing

Asking is simply asking students questions about topics other than their schoolwork. Examples would be asking about their weekend, their favorite band, or where they got their cool t-shirt. You follow this up with a genuine interest. I would ask students to borrow a CD of the band they liked and then make an effort to listen to it and talk about it with them. If I noticed them reading a book, I would attempt to read it as well so I knew what was interesting to them. Or if they said they had a bad weekend, I would follow up a few days later to make sure everything was alright. Asking questions of students not only helps you to know them better and form a better relationship, it makes students feel special.

Listening is another important factor in showing students you care. In the traditional classroom, students are not allowed to talk much, unless it is to provide answers to a question the teacher has posed; yet, students want to be heard. I cannot tell you the countless number of times that students have shared a story that has nothing to do with what we are talking about, and yet I have listened to them finish, rather than interrupting them. The listening needs to be intentional in that you are truly hearing what they have to say rather than trying to get the lesson back on track. Too often, students feel as though they don't have a voice. Your classroom needs to be a place where they feel they do.

Sharing is a third part of this equation. What is meant by this is sharing a little bit about yourself and what goes on in your life. Sometimes it feels as though kids think we live at the school and have no existence outside of it. I always chuckle at the look on their face when I run into a student at the grocery store. It's alright to share things about yourself to students. You don't have to get into your nitty gritty, personal life, or Facebook friend them, but sharing information about yourself such as your hobbies and interests, how you spent your weekend, your favorite sports team, or stories about your children (if you have them) can make students feel more connected to you. It makes you more than a robot whose directive is to give them lessons. It makes you a human being.

As a footnote, the student who told me I didn't do any of the 101 caring acts was with me for seventh and eighth grade. Then, he voluntarily came to my humanities program when he was a junior and senior. We became very close, and I wrote his letter of recommendation when he went to college. Years after he graduated, we still get together.

Visible Learning

Henry Wadsworth Longfellow summed it up nicely in his poem *The Arrow and the Song:*

> I shot an arrow into the air,
>
> It fell to earth, I knew not where;
>
> For, so swiftly it flew, the sight
>
> Could not follow it in its flight.

This is what it looks like in the classroom if you do not make it clear to students where the learning is going. Students will lose sight of what it is they are supposed to be learning. You have to make it transparent on a daily basis. If they cannot follow the flight of where your lesson is going, they are going to become disengaged and lose interest.

Why is this clarity so important? Do students need to know why they are learning something, or do they just need to be learning it? When John Hattie looked at over 800 meta-analyses related to achievement, the strategy near the very top was teacher clarity (Hattie, 2009).

Figure 2.1 *Effect Size of Teacher Clarity*

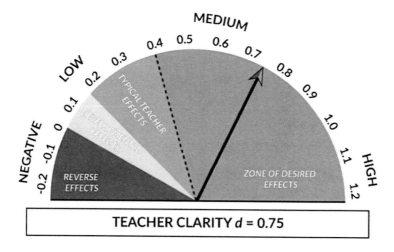

TEACHER CLARITY *d* = 0.75

You can see in the graphic above that teacher clarity has twice the effectiveness of typical teacher effects. When lessons are visible so that students know what they are learning and why they are doing so, their chances of learning go up exponentially. Not only that, when Scott Titsworth and his colleagues followed up Hattie's research with two meta-analyses of their own, the effects of teacher clarity were staggering (Titsworth et al., 2015). The first meta-analysis showed:

> 0.72 on academic learning

That falls where Hattie had placed it as well. The more interesting effect though was:

> 1.21 on student motivation and attitudes

Holy crap. Making your lessons visible so that they are clear causes students to be motivated. Imagine that.

You would think this would simply be common sense, but I have been in too many classrooms where a student asks, "Why are we learning this?" and the response the teacher gives is, "Because you'll need it for next year." That is a really crappy answer—certainly not inspiring in any way. If a teacher cannot give students a good reason why they are learning something, maybe they shouldn't be learning it?

But hold on. In the second meta-analysis performed by Titsworth et al. (2015), the results of teacher clarity were even more impressive:

> 1.02 on academic learning
>
> 1.25 on student motivation and attitudes

In seeing the effect teacher clarity has on student learning and motivation, it seems obvious that all teachers should be using this strategy in the classroom.

With that being said, what does teacher clarity look like? Let me provide you with an example of what it does *not* look like to provide context. In a classroom that lacks clarity, students may be confused about what they are learning. If you went around and asked students what they are learning, they would be able to tell you the activities they have been engaged in, but if you were to ask these students why they are doing these activities, the water becomes a little muddy.

I will give you an example from my own teaching experience. I was teaching a math unit to third and fourth graders on perimeter. In order to get them interested about it, I had them work on a project in which they designed a fort. I figured this would get them excited about perimeter, and they could use their imagination to boot. Much to my delight, students did get excited about the lesson. They dreamed up forts with trampoline rooms, basketball courts, fire poles, and rooms for their stuffed animals. To further challenge my students, I told them they had the opportunity to make a 3-D model of their fort. They could use Legos, sugar cubes, toothpicks, or any material they wanted. One student of mine came into class carrying a fort he had made out of popsicle sticks. It was the coolest model of a fort I had ever seen; it had an indoor pool, a tennis court, and a video game room for all of his consoles. I was so happy to see how proud of the model he was with his smile.

I said to him, "This is so amazing. What is its perimeter?"

Suddenly, the smile disappeared, only to be replaced by a look of panic.

"Uh, perimeter?" the student said nervously.

In my efforts to jazz up the lesson and make math more exciting for students, I had enabled this student to lose sight of what it was he was truly to be learning. How could he have worked for what seemed like weeks on a project, and not figured out what I had set out for him to learn in that time? Because my teaching lacked clarity. He was following an arrow as it flew into the air, but because he could not see the target, he could not follow its flight.

One way to develop clarity for learning in your classroom is by following these steps (Ainsworth, 2019):

1. Define and describe learning intentions and success criteria
2. Apply motivation to a single standard
3. Break a learning intention into learning progressions
4. Continue motivation with multiple standards within a unit of study
5. Co-construct success criteria
6. Transfer ownership of learning by partnering with students

The idea behind this is that you are making things as clear as possible for students and involving them in the process. It is not a coincidence that motivation appears twice in these steps. The more students are aware of what and why they are learning something, the more engaged and motivated they will be.

Student Choice

How often do we give students a choice in the classroom? Such choice can come in the form of what they are learning, how they will learn it, or how they are going to be assessed for mastery. By giving students choice, you show that you care about their opinion and needs. Many times, students feel as though they are not given any choice. It is always their parents, coaches, friends, or school making decisions for them. By providing something as simple as a menu board, students suddenly aren't being told what to do and have more control over their learning.

This doesn't mean your classroom becomes a free-for-all. You still have to manage students and provide structure. It just means to consider opportunities to offer choice within a lesson. For example, if you are asking students to respond to a prompt meant to show their ability to be persuasive, do they have to do so in writing? Could they give an oral answer or use some other artistic medium to show their ability to persuade?

Often in classes, students all take the same assessment. What if, instead, you gave students a choice as to how they could be assessed? It might look like this:

1. Demonstration
2. Electronic portfolio
3. Essay
4. Exhibition
5. Journal
6. Research paper
7. Presentation
8. Portfolio
9. Performance
10. Test (Stanley, 2014)

This way, students could find something that excites them or plays to their strengths. A student who is a strong writer might choose the essay or journal, while someone who likes to speak might take the presentation or performance option. Students who are tactile-kinesthetic might want to do a demonstration, while someone who enjoys technology might create an electronic portfolio. The end result is the same, however: students show mastery of their learning.

There are other ways to provide choice in the classroom, which will be discussed in Chapter Five, but some of these include homework, what resources they will use to learn, who they will be collaborating with, or how they will challenge themselves. You can even give them a simple choice, such as where to sit. This ability to choose makes students feel as though they have a voice in the class; as a result, they have more buy-in because they are part of the learning process. A classroom is not a dictatorship, contrary to some teacher beliefs; it is a partnership. When you provide students with a choice, they feel like a partner.

Authentic Learning

School can be a very sterile learning environment. Students complete worksheets, or work on problems, or write essays. These are turned into the teacher and graded, then they are handed back, and are either put up on the fridge or tossed in the trash. It reminds me of a story I heard involving the Great Depression. In order to provide work for people, the workers on the first shift would come in and dig a hole. When the second shift workers came in, they were told they needed to fill the hole. This repeated day after day. The point is that this was not authentic work. It was just the perception of work.

Same goes with schools. We have students work on something that helps them to learn, but is it authentic work? How enthused are students going to be knowing that what they are turning in is only going to be seen by the teacher and eventually end up in a landfill? What if there were another audience—an authentic audience—that was seeing their work? Wouldn't this cause them to care more about their work because someone other than the teacher would be looking at it? Wouldn't they be more motivated to perform better?

In order to help students care about what they are doing, there has to be some relevance to it. They need to feel a connection to it. What better way to do this than to make what they are doing authentic? This authenticity can come in many forms, whether it is working on a problem that really exists, looking at real cases they can apply to their situation and learn from, or creating a product that could actually be used in the real world.

Here is a simple way you can take a math assignment and make it have more of a real-world connection. If you are trying to show students how to add and subtract using decimals, you could give them problems like these:

1. $6.789 + 122.9$

2. $94.78 - 7.0284$

Students would have to line up the decimals and make sure they include all of the digits. This activity is certainly teaching them how to add and subtract decimals, but is it showing them how they will encounter decimals in the real-world? What if, instead, they worked on a problem like this?

> Your mom gives you $20 to go to the movies. She says you need to bring home at least $5 in change. Your ticket to the movie is $7.25. How much money do you have to spend at the concession stand, and what is the most you could purchase?

Soda – Medium	$4.23
Soda – Small	$3.72
Popcorn – Medium	$5.61
Popcorn – Large	$8.02

| Skittles | $2.68 |
| Nachos | $4.84 |

The likelihood that your students might be put into a situation similar to this in real life is pretty high. Students are seeing how decimals come into play in the real world; as a result, they are more likely to understand how the knowledge of being able to add and subtract decimals will be of use to them in an authentic situation.

Anytime you can make the lesson authentic, either through the topic, method of learning, the assessment, or the audience, it is going to help students to understand the context of what they are learning. They will see how what they are doing can be used in their lives, which makes what they are learning relevant; thus, they care more about it and will be more motivated.

Effective Management

If you are going to change the culture of motivation in your classroom, you are also going to have to change the way you run your classroom. There are a few things you may have to consider doing differently than the traditional manner:

- Classroom setup
- Grading/assessment
- Role of the student
- Role of the teacher

Consider not setting up your classroom in the traditional manner, or what I call the cemetery configuration. This is a classroom with the teacher desk at the front of the room, with all student desks pointed toward the front, just like tombstones in a cemetery. Ninety percent of the classrooms I go into are set up like this.

Why consider something different? Because the set-up of your classroom reflects the type of teaching you are more likely to do. The cemetery configuration lends itself to lecture and teacher-led lessons. If you are going to make your classroom one that is more student-led, such as one in which students are going to be working in groups often, you need to have desks where they can circle up or push desks together. If there is going to be a lot of discussion or debate, you would need to have desks on two sides of the room facing each other.

There has been a movement in schools lately to use flexible seating. This can take many forms, whether it be:

- Stools
- Exercise balls
- Cushions or mats
- Couches/futons
- Standing desks
- Low tables

The important thing is to find the set-up that works best with your teaching style, what works well with your students' learning styles, and how you intend to personalize the learning. It might also be a good idea to have seating that allows for all sorts of different configurations. If you are going to be open-minded about your teaching, you should do the same in the set-up of your classroom.

> **For further explanation, watch a video tutorial at https://youtu.be/IKsgVOSSy7M.**

Grading and assessment might look very different in this sort of classroom. Let's say you are doing project-based learning with a classroom full of tenth graders. Everyone is studying something different, everyone has made different choices in regard to product, and everyone is working at a different pace. The traditional manner of covering material at the pace of the entire class and then taking an assessment at the end of the lesson might not be the best fit.

When I was teaching fifth and sixth grade science, I divided the class into six units that covered all of the material I was required to for the year, taking the learning objectives directly from the Next Generation Science Standards and using some above-grade-level standards to challenge students. I posted these on a bulletin board in the classroom. On the first day of school, I told students, "You have 180 days to learn everything that is up on that bulletin board." I explained to them further they could go in any order they wanted, they could choose the assessment they would use to show me what they learned, and that students would be finishing at different times, meaning that not a single person in the class would be at the same place at the same time.

What this also meant was that because every student might be choosing a different sort of assessment, I couldn't have one single way to grade them. Thus, students were required to create their own rubric before beginning each unit. If a student chose to give a presentation to the class, he would create a rubric that would evaluate this type of performance assessment. If another student decided to demonstrate her own experiment, her rubric would have to reflect what this looked like when done well.

If you walked into my classroom, it looked like chaos. Organized chaos, but chaos nonetheless. Everyone was doing something different, some might be researching while others were physically constructing their products, while others were presenting their performance assessments. It was the most scary and hectic year I ever taught, but it was also the most fulfilling. If I had to pick 1 year that I felt was my best as a teacher, that would be the one. And ironically, I did less direct instruction than any other year I have been in education.

I had to be creative with my grade book, however. Because different kids were completing their units at different times, one student's report card might reflect a grade in ecosystems and thermal energy, while another student might just be renewable resources. I also got into the habit of not just grading the end product, but having formative assessments throughout to chart progress the student was making. This was typically done through the informal conferences I held with students.

The role of the student may look a lot different in your classroom as well. In a traditional classroom environment, the teacher is the one delivering content or guiding discussion, while the student assumes a passive role. This changes in this type of classroom, so that the student is doing most of the heavy lifting. The student is making choices and pursuing things he is genuinely interested in; therefore, he must take the initiative to direct his own learning. That means not waiting for the teacher to tell him what to do. Instead, the student has to figure out for himself how to learn, thus creating self-sufficient, independent learners.

The role of the teacher shifts in this sort of learning environment too. Instead of being the one who is dictating what is going to be done, you are making sure students are aware of the choices available to them. You will spend more of your time managing and organizing the classroom, rather than teaching it. Like any good manager, you need to make sure your workers have the resources needed to complete their work, that you are there to help them should they get stuck on anything, and that you are checking progress throughout, both up close and from afar. You check this progress by having conversations with your students about their work. This is something that almost never happens in a traditional classroom. Imagine being able to talk to your students one-on-one or in small groups on a daily basis.

Reflection

This phase is something we don't do enough of in our classrooms; thoughtful reflection upon what was learned. Typically, students take an assessment covering certain material, the assessment is graded and handed back, and then the class moves on to the next lesson. We are missing a valuable opportunity to find out what students truly learned. This is far more valuable than any answers students put on a test. This shows us what was valuable for them in the lesson, giving us information that helps us to guide our own practice. It also gives you good information on what your students find of value, another source for tapping into their personalized learning and getting your students motivated.

A reflection requires something that a lot of teachers think they don't already have enough of: time. It requires that the class stops for a moment and takes a breath. Some may feel that this is a waste of valuable class time, but how many times in your own life has such an action been a huge benefit? Shouldn't we take time to deduce what the takeaways were from the lesson before plowing into the next topic? This is where you will identify where the enduring understanding is taking place. What are students remembering about a lesson? What are they forgetting?

There are many different protocols for reflection, so choose the one that works best for your motives and what you'd like to discern from your students. No matter which one you choose, the main thing you can provide is space—both physically and mentally. The physical space means letting students spread out around the room and talk with others. Depending on their age, it might be letting students go on a walkabout, strolling around the school or its grounds, while pondering reflection questions you have provided or ones they have come with on their own.

You also need to provide a mental space for students to explore their feelings. This involves creating a classroom environment where it is perfectly acceptable and somewhat expected that students do this. That means modeling for students and providing a safe place where students aren't going to feel as though others will judge them, or that the teacher is going to admonish them for speaking their mind. Of course, you want to make sure this feedback is actionable. I always tell students when reflecting, you are more than welcome to tell me that this lesson sucked, but make sure you also include *why* it sucked so that I can learn from this.

An example of a reflection protocol that I like to use with students is called the snapshot protocol. You put students in groups and ask them to come up with three snapshots. A snapshot is defined as a still-life, with people representing whatever it is the scenario has called for. I usually ask students to provide me with a snapshot of the three most valuable things they learned during our unit, academically, personally, and collaboratively.

Here are some photos I took of teachers I was working with in a workshop on project-based learning using the snapshot protocol. The protocol called for them to create three snapshots: one representing what projects would look like perfectly executed in your classroom, what would be your worst nightmare, and what is more realistic, but you would take it.

Your worst nightmare:

Perfect situation:

Not perfect, but you'll take it:

I like this particular reflection protocol for a few reasons. First, it allows students to be creative. Students must come up with a still-life that represents the idea they want to convey. It is literally a case of a picture being worth a thousand words, so what are they going to put into their picture to show this? Second, it allows students to be active. Many students spend the entire day in a sedentary position, sitting at their desk. As frequently as possible, I like to provide activities that are going to allow students to get out of their seats and physically do something. Lastly, it provides a window into their hopes and fears from the lesson. It shows you what they value and most importantly, what motivates them. Your students will also provide you with a lot of food for thought with their snapshots.

I do not use the same protocol after every single lesson. Part of the art of this phase of motivation is finding the reflection that will produce the most thoughtful and helpful information. I will discuss different sorts of protocols for reflection in that chapter, but the main goal of them is to allow students to have a safe environment in which to share their thoughts and feelings. This doesn't necessarily have to be at the end of a lesson, either. You could do a reflection at the halfway point to see how progress is going, or even at the beginning in order to understand their preconceived notions.

Finding the Heart of It

If you create a culture of motivation in your classroom, students will be more engaged because you are allowing them to be invested in their learning. You do this by providing them with choice, showing that you care, and giving them more of the responsibility of learning.

Motivation is only part of the equation. Once you have students motivated, you need to teach them the habits that allow them to be successful. It is these habits that I will discuss at length in the next six chapters.

HOW THE HELL DO WE MOTIVATE THESE KIDS?

Chapter 3

CARING

"Every kid is one caring adult away
from being a success story."
- Josh Shipp

The first—and perhaps most important—part of motivating a child is caring about them. Why is this so important? Because students will work a hell of a lot harder for a teacher that they think cares about them than one who does not. Even though there are many different causes for lack of motivation, they usually have one commonality: someone's lack of caring. If a student's home life is tough, maybe it is a parent who does not care. Boredom is caused by teachers who do not care enough about their craft to make things engaging. A student might be surrounded by peers who do not care about school. I observe a lot of classrooms, and the correlation between how much a teacher cares compared with how much the students care is very apparent.

For example, I once observed a Calculus class. Within 5 minutes, it was clear that this teacher really cared about math. More importantly, when I looked around the room, the students seemed to care as well, asking thought-provoking questions, having rapport with the teacher, and the level of engagement. I went to another class with many of the same students, but they almost immediately pulled out their phones, put in earbuds, and were generally off-task. When this teacher went to teach, he went through the motions and was organized, but he did not seem to care very much about his topic. The first teacher seemed to care more—not just about the subject area, but also about his students. Over by his desk were the pictures of hundreds of students. He used something called Student of the Day, where he would read answers someone had provided at the beginning to the year about him/herself, and then the class would guess who it was. He also seemed familiar with their strengths and weaknesses in his interactions with them. I saw none of this in the other class.

Two Aspects of Caring

There are two sides of the coin when it comes to showing you care: academic and social/emotional. Academic caring means that you care about the subject area you are teaching. This does not mean that you are expert on what you are teaching, but simply that you give special attention to this subject area and demonstrate its importance in your actions. You can see this in an elementary classroom when a teacher must teach all subject areas, but one is her favorite or least favorite. There were six elementary schools in our district, and I was always surprised how high the social studies scores were for one of the buildings. Investigating a little further, in talking with the teacher, I could see how passionate she was about social studies. Yet, in other elementary buildings, it was presented as more of a chore than a chance to learn. She cared about her subject area, and the students paid this in kind with high test results.

Think back to the teachers who were the most inspirational for you as a student. I would stand to reckon that this person had a passion for the subject he/she was teaching, and this passion infected you as well. That's what caring about your subject area can do for students. In my own high school days, math and I had a hate/hate relationship. I hated doing it and hated being made to take math classes. The teachers I had my sophomore and junior years didn't help my attitude. One was so droll and uninspiring that I spent most of my time trying to find ways to sleep in his class. Imagine the teacher from *Ferris Bueller's Day Off,* and that paints a pretty good picture, only more boring. I barely escaped these classes with a D average, and I dreaded my senior year, which would be spent learning Calculus, one of the most difficult fields of math.

Luckily for me, my Calculus teacher was Mr. Goodrich. He was an older man with a red beard, and he really loved math. He got excited about it and loved diving into a problem. This excitement rubbed off on me, and I did something I hadn't done since the sixth grade: I cared about math. As a result, my grade for the year was an A. What had this teacher, whose class I should have been terrible in due to my disdain for the subject area and my history of poor math results, done that was different than the half a dozen teachers I had previously? He simply cared.

This also means caring about your craft of teaching. Are lesson plans ready to go when students walk into the room? Are you organized, with available resources that students may need to work on a lesson or making sure things go as planned? Are you professional in each and every way in the classroom?

Why is it so important to come off as a professional? Because it means students can count on you. I remember one time we had something scheduled, but things went wrong, and we had to resort to Plan B, which I had already planned out. One of my students said to me upon learning of the change in plans, "I knew you'd take care of it." This faith that she put in me meant the world. It meant that she saw me as being someone in her life who would take care of her, even if it was just in the classroom. There are a lot of students who don't feel they have someone who cares for them. A student believing someone is in their corner can make a difference in their life.

In my own classroom, I felt there were three things I could do to show I cared.

1. Be prepared
2. Care about my subject area

3. Provide them with choice

One of those things was to be prepared. That meant whenever I was presenting a lesson or starting a project, I had done the work ahead of time. I know this seems obvious, but ask your students if they have ever had a teacher who made them wait while he or she gets things ready. You'll be surprised. Part of that preparedness is being organized as well. I am not terribly organized in my personal life, but I am very organized in the classroom. The main reason for this is that I want to set a good example. If I am expecting students to be organized, I should expect the same of myself. In addition, studies show that if a teacher is unorganized, this can cause students to follow suit, and even affect behavior. I want to make sure students know I care about the classroom and their time, just as I would expect them to do the same.

Caring about my subject area is also important. Ask anyone in my family, and they will tell you that I am no math expert, or even a novice at that. And yet, when I taught in a gifted pull-out program for third and fourth graders, one of the subject areas I had to teach was math. I had to make sure students were not aware of my disdain of math, because this could rub off on them. I had to demonstrate the value of math so that they thought of it as being important. I am always surprised by the power a teacher has to influence children. If I came into a lesson showing them that I don't care for math, they might adopt that same attitude.

A good part of my career was spent teaching history, but the bulk of this time was spent learning about it. The more I learned, the more I could bring to my lessons. There were times when we were covering a topic that wasn't so exciting to me, such as the Indus River Civilization. Instead of begging this off, I learned everything I could about the ancient civilization, eventually stumbling upon something that I found interesting that I could get excited about with kids—in this case, its grid planned cities.

The third thing I could do to show I cared was to give students opportunities to do things they cared about. This mostly came in providing them with choice. This will be discussed more in a later chapter, but knowing they have some say in the class and that they are not always being told what to do, is an indication to students that you care about their thoughts and opinions.

What can you do to let students know that you care about them and about your teaching? I think Jose Vilson said it best when he claimed the five things you can do to let students know that you care for them:

1. Show them.
2. Show them.
3. Show them.
4. Show them.
5. Show them. (Vilson, 2014, p. 23)

As simple as that sounds, I do want to provide you with a few simple strategies that you can use in your classroom to show your students you care.

Try to Have Conversations Whenever Possible

It can be tough to have a one-on-one conversation with a student when you have 30 kids in your classroom. One prime opportunity is that time between when the bell rings, sending kids from your class and bringing others in, to the time when class starts. Rather than have superficial platitudes such as "How are you doing?" or "Did you have a good weekend?" with dozens of students, pick one student a day to strike up a conversation with. This means asking them questions that will spark a true conversation, rather than a dead-end question.

Some questions you could ask students include:

1. What was the best part about your day?
2. What work is most exciting to you this week?

3. What new ideas are giving you energy lately?

4. Tell me one thing you've learned recently that inspired you.

5. What is one thing we could do right now to make this (day, project, event) even better? (Ludema, 2018, para. 7)

These questions will cause students to pause and consider their answer, requiring more than a simple yes or no. These questions will provoke a conversation that you can have in the 5 minutes before the bell rings. Make sure you rotate the students you are talking to and engage with students who normally wouldn't be outgoing or talkative. You don't have to single them out across the classroom, but going over and having a chat with them shows that you care about them as a person.

What I loved to do in my classroom was get students independently working on a project and then take that opportunity to move around the room, sit down with a student, and begin asking them about their project. These conversations served two purposes: one, I discovered more about what my students were learning, and two, students could see that I cared about them as individuals, rather than just another group of students in my class.

Be a Good Listener

A second thing you can do to show students you care for them is to be a good listener. In the role of the teacher, we often end up doing most of the talking, not taking the time to listen to what students have to say. This is all about giving students a voice, which Rebecca Coda and Rick Jetter (2018) discussed in their book *Let Them Speak!* There are three different levels of listening:

Level 1: We get in tune with our own thoughts, opinions, and judgments: We might be asking ourselves, "What would I have done in this situation?" "What does this remind me of?" or "How does what this person is saying pertain to me?" "How can I get back on track?" You know when you're with someone and they seem to be sort of half listening? Or listening to respond with their own tidbit of information? Yeah, that's not fully listening.

Level 2: We recognize the tone, pace, energy, and agenda of the other person. With this level, we don't just listen to the words, but also the expression, the emotion, the tone, the speed, and the body language (if you are privy to it) that goes along with the words. You even listen to the hesitations and what's not said. So, imagine you ask a child "how are you?" and the child answers "fine." When we are listening on Level 2, we might note that their answer is full of contentment, sadness, frustration, or fear. In that case, "fine" might mean "good;" to the 'in-tune' listener, however, it might mean anything from "I feel lonely" to "I'm hurt, but don't want to tell anyone."

Level 3: We use our intuition, the information feeding into the environment around us, and the multiple factors that are impacting the conversation at any given time. This is 360-degree global listening. It takes practice. With Level 3 listening, your gut fills in the story, and you start to gain a fuller understanding of the person in front of you. You take in consideration everything around you. Is the other person fulfilled? Annoyed? Blocked? Level 3 listening, used in tandem with Level 2 listening, is about nuances and what's beyond words. It often tells more than the words can ever do on their own. When we really listen, we can pick up on this stuff.

Many times, early in my career I listened to what students had to say at Level 1. Especially the part about how I was just waiting until they were finished to tell them what I thought, rather than actively listening. I know what a lot of teachers are thinking while reading this: "I would love to listen at Level 3, but I don't always have the time to do so." If you want to show students that you care, you should find the time. I found that listening closely to them—and not being so quick to give my teacherly advice—saved me time because I was creating a relationship with them where I could ask open and honest questions and expect those types of answers in return.

How exactly do you get to Level 3 of listening? There are several strategies; however, here are a few suggested by *Forbes* magazine for leaders, which I think is very appropriate for the classroom teacher:

1. **Engage yourself:** Find out what is important to your students and ask them questions about it and encourage them to share more. Make it about them and not yourself.

2. **Be empathetic:** Show your students that you feel their frustrations. A student might have broken a school rule, but might have had what to them was a justified reason for doing so. Rather than being so quick to punish, try to get their side of the story. You might still end up punishing them, but at least they felt you listened to them.

3. **Don't judge:** When you judge, you are not listening. Try listening to what a student is saying without judgement. Let them tell their side of the story.

4. **Be mindful:** This means listening to more than just their words. Are you paying attention to body language, facial expressions, and other non-verbal communication? A student may say they are doing fine, but their behavior might indicate otherwise. Are you looking at all of the signs?

And, of course...

5. **Show that you care:** This takes care of itself if you are doing the other four. Drawing that line between student and teach-

er can be very tricky at times, but just because the bell rings, doesn't mean the caring stops. Have lunch with your students for time to time, offer your class up for extracurricular activities before or after school (e.g., chess club, board games, ping pong), and make sure you check your email periodically during the evening. I know some teachers have a strict "I'm done with work" policy and don't check their school email once the school day is complete, but a student might have a question about an assignment or be unsure about something, and you have the ability to set their mind at ease and show you care (Llopis, 2013).

Make Them Part of the Learning Process

Part of this listening can be considering student voice into the learning. Throughout their schooling career, students have very little choice in what they learn. The content is determined by the curriculum, and the method used to learn is decided by the teacher. What if you allowed students to be part of this process?

For example, because I have a lot of performance-based assessment in my classroom, I use rubrics as a tool to capture what students have learned. For years, I simply made the rubric and handed it to the students at the beginning of the lesson. I noticed two things about this process. One, students rarely took the rubric out during the course of the lesson. No matter how many times I told them this served as a blueprint for how to get a good grade, not many students would refer to it. When I saw them heading down a wrong path, I would ask to see their rubric to get them back on track, and it was often buried in a folder somewhere—or, worse, could not be found. The second thing I noticed is after spending a lot of time using the rubric to grade them, giving tons of feedback with which to improve next time, most kids would simply glance at the grade and then either throw it in the trashcan or leave it behind when they left for their next class.

Then I realized I was missing a great opportunity to let students have some say in how they are graded. What I began to do was when introducing a lesson, I would talk about what students would need to produce to show mastery of the learning. Sometimes this was an essay, other times a research paper, presentation, or demonstration. Regardless of what it was, why couldn't the students have some say in what this would look like if it were done at a high level? Didn't they have numerous experiences they could bring to the table as examples of what to do and what not to do?

We began to make the rubrics as a class. I would take a blank rubric and together we would fill in the blanks of what it looked like at various levels of mastery. Occasionally, I would wordsmith a description or make a suggestion of my own, but most times the students were making all of the decisions. What was really interesting is that the students usually arrived at nearly the exact same rubric I would have handed them, but because they had been engaged in the process, they had more ownership for the expectations and were more aware of them. I began to see more students using the rubric throughout the lesson, but even those who did not were more familiar with it because they had helped to construct it.

As for handing the rubrics back, I decided to have a conversation with them, rather than just putting it on their desk. I would get together with individual students or a group if it had been a collaborative effort, and ask them this question, "What would you have given yourself if you were me?" Students would then tell me the grade they thought they deserved. When I first began to do this, I fully expected students to claim they all deserved As, but I found the exact opposite to be the truth. Most students were much harder on themselves that I had been. There were times, however, where a student would make a good argument for why they deserved a better grade than I had given them; if they had a legitimate point, I would raise their grade. This was yet another example of how students played a role in their learning process. Through this reflection process, they learned where I was coming from and got to be part of the conversation.

By making them part of the learning process, I showed that I care about their voice, and as an extension of that, that I care about them. I began to take this even further in my classroom after seeing such positive results, incorporating inquiry-based lessons into my classroom. If we had to learn about the American Revolution, rather than me telling kids what they were going to be learning, I gave them a choice in the matter. I gave them a brief overview such as the causes, who were the important people, and what events were often remembered. Then, I let students pick one aspect of the American Revolution that they found interesting and challenged them to become an expert about it. They were tasked with teaching the other members of the class about this topic in depth. When a couple of students or more chose the same topic, this organically became a group and they worked together.

I had more students caring about the American Revolution than I had ever had before. The reason for this was my giving them enough respect and care to trust them to choose what they were going to learn. They were learning for the love of learning, not because something was assigned to them.

Be Vulnerable

This does not mean to share your innermost feelings or being willing to cry. It means coming off as a human being. Make sure students know who you are. You don't have to share your deepest, darkest secrets, but letting them know you have a family or pet, expressing interests such as sports or hobbies, or sharing something you did over the weekend can let students in. It can be as simple as having photos of family members on your desk, the pennant of the school you graduated from, or a poster of a professional team you live and die for. It does not mean being social media friends with them (I have a strict policy that I don't accept these until after they have graduated) or giving them your cell number and talking with them after school hours. There are certainly lines you do not want to cross, and you want to maintain your professionalism. It just means opening yourself up to them a little bit.

I think the best way you can show students that you are vulnerable is being willing to admit to your mistakes. Some students are sitting there, waiting for you to make a mistake so that they may pounce on it. This could be misspelling a word on the board or having an error on an assignment. Rather than get defensive or try to deflect the criticism, lean into it. Admit to the mistake and show students that you know you are not perfect. I got to the point where I would purposely make a typo on an assessment and made it a contest as to who could find it first. This did two things. It made them read the assessment very carefully and would help their comprehension. It also showed them that mistakes are just a part of life, and that I could make them too.

We often say that our classrooms are a place where students should feel safe to make mistakes. I think we need to extend this courtesy to ourselves as teachers. Not everything is going to go perfectly every time. By being able to acknowledge this, we can serve as a model for students that failure is perfectly acceptable. It is this failure which pushes your limits and teaches you far more than any successes. This is the type of failure which can result in a life-long lesson of great significance.

An example from my own classroom was when I was teaching sixth graders about Ancient Greece. I decided to do a project, and it went about as poorly as you could imagine. Students were not understanding what they were supposed to be learning, and their products were inferior as a result. After the project was over, I felt I had failed my students by not having a good structure or a clear goal to which students could aspire. I asked my students to put their chairs in a circle and admitted as much to them. Then I pleaded with them for recommendations of I could make it better for next year's class.

My students responded to my being vulnerable with them and admitting my mistakes by helping me redesign the project complete with a product and a good idea of the rubric. Together, we learned that a mistake is not a mistake if we can learn from it and make it better. That was just what we did, as I used their project idea the following year to great success.

Finding the Heart of It

Showing students that you care should be a no-brainer, and anyone entering the field of education more than likely cares for children; otherwise they would not take on such a demanding profession. The issue is that it doesn't work if we are the only ones who know that we care for our students. It must be transparent and seen on a daily basis how you care about your subject area, how you care about the profession, and most importantly, how you care about your students. The only way they are going to know this is if you show them. You will find that students are going to be more motivated about school and doing well if they are in a classroom where they feel cared for.

HOW THE HELL DO WE MOTIVATE THESE KIDS?

Chapter 4
VISIBLE LEARNING

"In an effective classroom, students should not only know what they are doing. They should also know how and why."
- Brian Tracy

How often for a vacation do people get in the car and say, "I'm just going to go where the road takes me?" Almost never, because they would waste time getting to somewhere they didn't want to go. This is how some kids feel about school. Because the teacher has not made clear what they are learning, or why they are learning it, they feel like they are just wandering around aimlessly. That is why visible learning is so important. When you get in that car to go on vacation, you want to aim that thing towards a place you would like to go.

Clarity of Learning

In order to achieve clarity of learning, you need to start with teacher clarity. The question becomes, what is clarity? In its simplest form, teacher clarity means communicating to students *what* they are learning, *how* they will be learning it, and *why* they will be learning it.

Almarode and Vandas (2018) described four areas that need to be covered to make sure students are clear on the purpose of their learning:

- Gaining clarity
- Sharing clarity

- Feedback with clarity
- Assessing with clarity

Each of these will be discussed in further detail throughout the chapter.

Gaining Clarity

In order to be able to teach something, it is first necessary to understand it. This seems like common sense, but I am sure there have been times when you are not entirely sure what a content standard is asking because its description is vague. Or maybe you are teaching a subject area that is not necessarily your strong suit. I am licensed by the state of Ohio to teach psychology to high school students, but I would be way out of my element if asked to helm such a class. I have certainly had to teach topics in social studies classes that I did not have a good understanding of at first. My first assignment as a teacher was five classes of ancient history, from prehistoric man to the age of discovery. This was a bit of a challenge because my focus in college had been American History. I did not have a firm grasp on what Mesopotamia was or why it was referred to as the cradle of civilization. I was learning right along with the students, so how on earth could I have provided them with any clarity when I didn't possess it myself?

Sometimes, it is not just the content which is not being fully addressed; it could be the level of thinking the standard is asking for students to demonstrate in order to show mastery. When we look at content standards, we as teachers need to unpack them for two things: content and level of thinking. The content of the standard is contained within the noun of the standard. Take for example this Common Core Standard for grade 6:

> Write, read, and evaluate expressions in which letters stand for numbers.

When you look at the noun, this is learning about expressions in which letters stand for numbers. But if you look at the verbs, they tell you which levels of thinking you should be able to do this. It is about being able to:

1. Write
2. Read
3. Evaluate

There would be many teachers that would teach their students to read and write expressions in which letters stand for numbers and think they were done with this standard. This would be applying the skill, but one of the verbs also asks students to be able to evaluate, which is a higher level of thinking. If a teacher is not teaching students all three of these skills or putting students in situations where they get to use all three skills, then the standard is not being covered with clarity.

As teachers, it is our duty to make sure we are clear in what it is we are supposed to be teaching students so that they may be clear in the manner in which they learn it. In succinct terms, you have to make sure you've got it before you can expect your students to get it as well.

Sharing Clarity

Once we have achieved this clarity, the trick becomes how to most effectively share it with others. There are a few strategies that you can use to share with students what they will be learning. The purpose of all of these is to make your learning intentions clear. Learning intentions can focus on:

- Knowledge
- Skills
- Concepts

These are typically conveyed in the content standards provided by your school, state, or the Common Core Content Standards. The problem with these is that they are written by adults for teachers rather than in a kid-friendly language. For the example, take the following standard for ELA:

> With prompting and support, ask and answer questions
> about key details in a text.

This is written for a kindergarten student. Could you imagine putting this standard in front of a 6-year-old and it being clear to him or her what is supposed to be learned?

Let's unpack this standard and determine what it is that kindergarteners need to be learning using the nouns and verbs. The nouns of this standard are *details* and *text*. This is the content of the standard—that students will be able to read or have read to them a text and be able to remember the details. How can we write that in a way that makes sense to a 6-year-old? The verbs show the actions the students must take; they must *ask* and *answer*. These are two different actions, however. One way to write the standard in a more kid-friendly manner is to break it down into each of the actions required. Your standard might become:

> Ask questions about the story.
>
> Answer questions about the story.

By breaking it down, you can evaluate these skills separately. A student may be able to answer questions, but not ask them. Or, he might be able to ask questions, but not answer them. He might need more work on one more than the other. Breaking it down helps you as the teacher as well by understanding what students must do to achieve mastery.

Next, change these into "I can" statements. Putting it into this form shifts the learning into action and gives the student confidence that he/she can master it. It is the attainability piece of goal valuation. Much like the fabled story of the little engine who stated, "I think I can, I think I can," these words give students motivation to succeed.

Those statements from before simply get turned into "I can" statements by putting that phrase in front of them:

I can ask questions about the story.

I can answer questions about the story.

You can make it even more clear to students by defining the story. Let's say you have decided to read *Green Eggs and Ham* by Dr. Seuss to the class. The statements then become:

I can ask questions about *Green Eggs and Ham*.

I can answer questions about the story *Green Eggs and Ham*.

Now students know exactly what it is they need to do to show mastery of learning. There is no mystery to the purpose of them hearing this story. The purpose of hearing this story is to be able to ask and answer questions about it. That is clear to students right up front and guides them regarding what to listen for and pay attention to. Otherwise, if this is not clear, some students might pay attention to the colors on the pages, while others might focus on the unique vehicles shown in the story. This puts everyone on the same page, both figuratively and literally.

When it comes time to demonstrate mastery of the content standard, the students are very aware of what is expected of them. They will be answering questions the teacher asks about details in the story. They will also be expected to ask questions of their own. Not only is this clear to the students, it will be clear to the teacher so she knows what she will need to do in order for students to show mastery.

Don't assume this is only done at the lower levels of education. Juniors and seniors in high school need clarity of learning as well, especially because the content standards become so much more complex with every passing grade. For example, here is a math content standard from high school statistics and probability:

Recognize the purposes of and differences among sample surveys, experiments, and observational studies; explain how randomization relates to each.

There is a lot going on in this standard. Students may know what each of these words mean, but they are so densely packed together. First, consider the nouns:

Sample surveys, experiments, observational studies

Then, there are the adjectives that inform those nouns:

Purposes, difference, randomization

The student must know the purpose, difference, and randomization of each of the nouns. Students must be aware of the basic content in order to understand this, as well as to activate the verbs included which are:

Recognize, explain

When you unpack it and break it up, it becomes so much clearer to understand:

1. Recognize the purposes of sample surveys.
2. Recognize the purposes of experiments.
3. Recognize the purposes of observational studies.
4. Recognize the differences among sample surveys.
5. Recognize the differences among experiments.
6. Recognize the differences among observational studies.
7. Explain how randomization relates to sample surveys.
8. Explain how randomization relates to experiments.
9. Explain how randomization relates to each observational study.

See how much clearer these learning targets are. It lays all the learning out for both you and the students. A student cannot recognize the difference in sample surveys if she does not know how to read one.

A student cannot explain the purpose of observational studies if he does not know what they even are. The lower-level skills of recall and understanding must occur before students can get to the higher-level thinking of explaining.

If you were to throw this standard at a high school student and expect him to be clear on what he should be learning, you would have another thing coming. By breaking it down into "I can" statements, what the student is expected to learn becomes transparent:

1. I can recognize the purposes of sample surveys.
2. I can recognize the purposes of experiments.
3. I can recognize the purposes of observational studies.
4. I can recognize the differences among sample surveys.
5. I can recognize the differences among experiments.
6. I can recognize the differences among observational studies.
7. I can explain how randomization relates to sample surveys.
8. I can explain how randomization relates to experiments.
9. I can explain how randomization relates to each observational study.

By breaking it into nine parts, this also means you have to assess mastery nine different times. This could be addressed in a single project where students must employ all of these skills, a few formative assignments/assessments spread over a couple of weeks, or a summative assessment using numerous questions designed to allow students to show mastery in multiple forms. Assessing with clarity will be discussed in more detail later on in this chapter.

Another strategy to make the standard more clear is to rewrite the standard as an essential question. For instance, take a look at this Next Generation Science Standard for middle school students:

> Conduct an investigation to provide evidence that living
> things are made of cells; either one cell or many differ-

ent numbers and types of cells.

This could be boiled down into a single essential question that asks:

Do all living things have cells?

Within that essential question you would conduct your investigation, provide evidence, and differentiate between single celled creatures and multi-celled ones, but you are always answering the essential question.

To help you write your learning intentions in a language that kids can understand, enlist your students into helping to shape this essential question. This could be done in a class discussion; you could break them into small groups with the task of each group developing an essential question, or you could have students develop their own individual learning target and then hold them accountable to it. Getting students involved in the learning process helps them to better understand what it is they are supposed to be learning and helps you to be able to look at it from their perspective and put it in words that they will better understand. As a result, they will see the importance of it and thus be more motivated.

The learning targets should be visible throughout the classroom. This means it is written on the board; it is front and center on their papers or assignments; it is posted on your class webpage; and you remind them whenever you are addressing the class or talking with individual students. How do you know the students are clear on what it is they are supposed to be learning? An easy test of this would be if you asked any student in the classroom what she was learning and why, she should be able to provide you with an answer.

Feedback with Clarity

Once students understand what they need to do and are in the process of mastering the content standard, they need to receive feedback on what they are doing well, what they could improve, and how they can take it to the next level. This feedback needs to be conveyed clearly to students—in either written or verbal form, or both—and it needs to be done consistently throughout the lesson. If you wait until the summative assessment to provide feedback, it would be like telling a patient who is already on her deathbed how she could have avoided this. If you only provide them with feedback when work is for a grade, it is not going to be as effective; it can actually be detrimental. Black and William (2009) found that 60% of students made significantly greater improvements when feedback was not tied to a grade. You should be providing this feedback in a formative setting, meaning that it is ongoing and done while students are in the process of learning.

Researchers have shown that feedback is what leads to a clarity of learning for students. Marzano (2001) found an effect size for feedback of 0.76, which translates roughly into a 28% difference in average achievement. Hattie (2009) reported a similar effect size of 0.73 and ranked it among the highest of hundreds of educational practices that he studied.

Keep in mind that feedback is not micromanaging students and their work. Feedback is listening and observing your students work. It is offering suggestions or guidance to nudge them in the correct direction or to push them further. Moreover, feedback need not be formal. It could be something as simple as overhearing a conversation between a group of students and then asking a probing question designed to make them think about it a little differently. It might look something like this:

> **Student #1:** I don't agree with Hester Prynne's actions. I would have totally told everyone that Dimmesdale was the father.
>
> **Student #2:** Yeah, I wonder why she protected him?
>
> **Teacher:** But have you considered the Puritan setting of the book. How would you act if you were a Puritan in

the 1600s?

Then, the teacher walks away. This feedback is designed to extend the wonderful thinking the students are already doing, not correct it. Hopefully these two students will think about what the teacher suggested and consider its perspective, further extending their understanding.

You should definitely not provide feedback for feedback's sake. There is a wrong way to provide feedback. General statements or a pat on the back do nothing to advance the thinking or skill building of a student. Despite the generally beneficial effects of feedback, it can have a negative effect on learning if it lacks clarity (Shute, 2008). A lot of the time we equate feedback with criticism, that we only tell students what they are doing wrong. We need to point out when students are doing something right as well; this way, they can repeat this desired effect in the future. We should be specific about this feedback so that it is clear which action provided which positive result. It might look like this:

> **Teacher:** Tony, I really liked the presentation you gave.
>
> **Tony:** Thanks, Mr. Jenson.
>
> **Teacher:** The part I thought that was especially effective was when you showed that graphic of the cut-open bird who had died from ingesting plastic bottle rings. It really shocked me and caused me to be angry as those who had littered and killed that poor bird.
>
> **Tony:** I wasn't sure I was going to show it. I thought it might bother some people.
>
> **Teacher:** I think given the context of the topic of your presentation on pollution in our oceans, it was completely appropriate. You could hear the students gasp, but I think it was a gasp of shock that their pollution was causing this, not because it was a graphic photo.
>
> **Tony:** I'm glad I used it then.

This feedback will stick with Tony and give him something specific that he can carry over when doing something similar. If the teacher had simply left it at that he liked the presentation, Tony may never have figured out what was good about it or how effective his decision was.

In the movie *Whiplash*, the character played by J.K. Simmons says, "There are no two words in the English language more harmful than 'good job.'" To a certain extent, he is correct. Telling someone they did a good job without being clear what about the job was good doesn't help that student get any better. Although intended to make a student feel better about himself, it does not help him grow as a learner. Even worse is when a student does not do a good job, and yet we claim they did in order to boost them up. The message sent is that you can do substandard work and be complimented anyway. It does not result in better work.

Feedback also needs to be specific and actionable. What I mean by actionable is that the feedback provides students with some guidance or aims them toward a specific action they can take to make it better. For example, if a student is working on a set of math problems, and you see that he has made a mistake, rather than just telling him that it is wrong, coach him where he might have taken a misstep. It doesn't have to be as specific as, "You messed up right here," but should be designed to aim them in the correct direction such as, "You might want to check your fraction conversion."

I see instances of ineffective feedback all the time such as when teachers collect homework, check that it is done, and give it right back to the student. How on earth does this help this student? The entire purpose of homework is for students to practice their skills. There may be things wrong with the homework that the student now thinks is correct because he didn't receive any feedback to the contrary. Not only that, it devalues the work the student has done because she may have spent an hour working on it, only to have the teacher simply glance at it and mark it off as complete. If teachers are going to assign homework, they should be prepared to offer feedback, both written and spoken, on that homework in order to guide the student to greater success. It doesn't have to be a paragraph, but a little written comment that informs students and provides them with direction will be beneficial to their learning.

A strategy for written feedback might be you walking around the room and observing what students are doing with a pad of sticky notes in your hand. When you see something you would like to advise a student on or to encourage him to pursue further, write this feedback on the note and stick it to their desk. This way, you are not interrupting them, and they can refer to it at their own leisure. It might look like this:

I liked your idea of compairing the experiment to Darwin's. Explore that further.

Or this:

I noticed you are using Wikipedia for a lot of your sources. Make sure to explore the citations at the bottom of the article and explore those sources for more information.

Teachers are not makers of learners; we are shapers. This shaping is achieved through effective feedback. Look at it like you are smoothing off some rough edges, but the students are doing the bulk of the creating. Make your learning intentions clear and allow them to learn on their own with your guidance.

Assessing with Clarity

In a traditional classroom, the teacher provides information, the students learn this information, and the teacher assesses this on a summative assessment given at the end of the lesson. Hopefully from the last section you have discovered that this feedback needs to be ongoing. Although there will be many formative checks throughout this process, there will come a time when you will assess mastery. When this time occurs, you want to ensure that you are assessing this mastery with clarity.

What is not effective feedback is simply marking whether answers are correct or not, or when just a letter grade is given. I see this when a teacher returns a test back with just a grade or encouraging words that are not specific to anything. How is that going to help a student get better or realize what she did well and should continue to do? Even multiple-choice tests with their one correct answer can have effective and clear feedback. You could make comments on such things as...

- This one was wrong because...
- Your thinking was right on this one, but you made a silly mistake.
- Used good logic to figure one of the answers out.
- What might have been an even better answer but was not a choice?
- How do you think you would have reacted if it was you?
- Remember to use the _____ to solve this.
- How did you arrive at this answer?

There are all sorts of comments you can place on a multiple-choice test that would act as effective feedback that would help students learn better.

This goes for any assessments, whether it be a paper, an essay, a performance, or some other alternative assessment. I remember several times in my college career when I worked on a paper for not hours, but days. I put my blood, sweat, and tears into writing it, and I proudly turned it in to my teacher, only to receive it back a couple of weeks later with a single letter grade written in the upper right-hand corner, nothing else. I found this frustrating, even if the grade was an A, because I was given no indication as to why I deserved the grade I received. What did I do so well to receive this? And because there is no such thing as the perfect paper, there are still things that could have been improved or thought about in a different way. I would have appreciated that feedback because I could have used it to make my writing better. How difficult would it have been for that teacher while reading my paper to have put a note or two in the margins such as, "I like this vivid imagery you used" or "Make sure to avoid this run-on sentence." That would have been much more valuable than the uninformative grade attached to the paper.

It is not enough to say whether something was right or wrong, but providing feedback on what they did well or what they might be misunderstanding would be helpful to that student. When I would grade student performances using a rubric, I made sure to not just circle the part of the rubric that showed their level of mastery, but also why I placed it where I did. A graded rubric would look like this:

Figure 4.1 *5-Minute Speech Rubric*

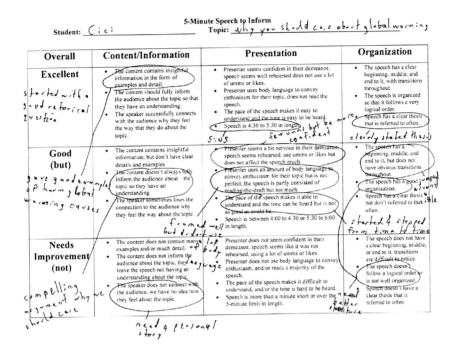

Notice that for every description I circled, I had an accompanying comment. Even the ones in the "excellent" range were informed why it was so excellent, while the "good" range comments were designed to show the student what she might have improved on. In addition to this written feedback, I made an effort to sit down with the student and talk about how I saw her performance as compared to her perception of it. I usually began the conversation with "How do you think you did?" just to get the student voice and then go from there, giving her as much specific feedback using the rubric as my guide to help her to improve or to realize what she performed well and should continue to do.

This was the sort of attention to feedback I gave to any student assessment, whether it be a written test, a product they produced, or something they performed. Keep in mind, I was giving them feedback formatively as they were working on it as well. Most times I knew what the summative was going to look like because I had been working with the student all along. Very rarely did a student produce something that wasn't what I had expected because I had been monitoring them along the way and making sure they were aimed in the correct direction.

Finding the Heart of It

Visible learning is probably one of the most effective strategies in students learning in your classroom. After all, they cannot learn when they don't know what it is they are supposed to be learning. This first starts with you, the teacher, and making sure you understand what it is they are supposed to be learning. Then it is successfully communicating that with your students. Next your role becomes that of the tour guide, pointing students in the right direction and correcting their course should they go astray. This guiding comes in the form of the feedback you provide students, not just on their assessments, but throughout the process. This is going to help with all three aspects of goal valuation:

> **Interesting:** When you take away the secretiveness of what they are learning and make clear to students what the plan is, they take more interest in it.

> **Importance:** By students seeing what the learning intentions are, they can see how it fits into the big picture of their learning and understand why it is relevant to learn. Connecting it to their own lives by showing how it will manifest itself in the real world will cause more students to see the importance of WHY they are learning what you are asking them to learn.

> **Attainable:** By being clear with learning expectations, students receive a roadmap for success. Because HOW you are going to assess mastery is made clear to them, they can see how to attain this level of success and what they are going to have to do. It no longer seems like an insurmountable challenge, but rather a pathway to learning.

As much as the research shows that providing clarity is an effective teaching practice, what also improves student achievement is the fact that your students are now more motivated, which is always going to make for better learning.

HOW THE HELL DO WE MOTIVATE THESE KIDS?

Chapter 5

STUDENT CHOICE

"Student choice is more than simply picking a task.
It's about owning the entire learning process."
- John Spencer

The idea of choice in creating a culture of motivation is simply about providing it. You want to be able to provide a range of options for students to choose from. Student choice can be a very powerful motivational tool. From the very earliest age, kids are told what to do, how to do it, and when they should do it. This comes from their parents, coaches, teachers, older siblings, and anyone else who is older than them and thinks they know better. It's what sucks about being a kid: you have to wait until you are an adult to get to make any choices for yourself.

The biggest obstacle to this is the way school is run. Schools should model what they are doing based on what the school cafeteria does. Let me be a little more clear about this so you don't think I'm suggesting we offer Bosco sticks and Big Daddy's pizza in all of our classrooms. Cafeterias in the 1970s worked like an assembly line. Students grabbed a tray and silverware, and were spoon-fed their meal, each portion going into the allotted spot on the tray. Students had no choice in what they were getting or how much of it. Their choice only came into play when sitting down to decide what out of these offerings they were willing to eat, throwing out what they deemed did not look appetizing.

This is also how classrooms looked in the 1970s. Students filed into class, sat in predetermined desks, and received the same lessons, textbooks, and assignments, which they had to complete at the same pace. The teacher then took all of this and assigned a grade. The only choice the students had was what they were and were not willing to learn.

School cafeterias today look very different from what they did 50 years ago. Most cafeterias have come to the conclusion that students need choice. This choice might be in the form of what entrée or sides they offer, the number of portions or amount, or even options such as having a salad, sandwich, international, or pasta bar. Why is there so much choice in the cafeteria? Because cafeterias have come to realize that specific students have specific needs. If you are giving green beans to every student who comes through the line, yet three out of every 10 students don't like them, you are wasting at least 30% of your content. It is impossible to meet the various needs of these students by offering them the same meal, so students can pick and choose which meal is most appealing to them. Because it is more appealing, they are more likely to actually consume the meal, ultimately reducing waste.

Does this make preparing meals more difficult? Sure it does. You have to prepare several meals now instead of just one. Then why make things more difficult for themselves? Because school cafeterias have come to the realization that the kids are their customers. And if the customer isn't happy, nobody is happy. Without choice, the kids aren't happy because they are being told what they have to eat, and the cafeteria workers are serving food students don't want—not a particularly inspiring environment. By offering various choices and putting the kids' needs first, the students are happy because they're getting food they enjoy eating, and the cafeteria workers see satisfied kids—a much more inspiring environment.

Teachers and educational leaders, on the other hand, have not reached this conclusion. They still think the teachers are the ones who should be calling the shots and making the decisions of what and how to learn something. It is still very much the 1970s school cafeteria model of, "This is the way I teach, and kids should have to figure out how to learn in this environment." Why has the cafeteria changed its ways, while the traditional classroom has not?

Just like the cafeteria, classrooms should be à la carte. Students come in with certain needs, likes, and tastes, and teachers should be offering them lessons that allow them to make choices that feed into these.

Children are drawn to hobbies and interests that provide them with some choice. I see my younger daughter watching YouTube constantly, and used to wonder why that is. Then I remembered when I was kid, I would get up every Saturday morning before anyone else and watch 4 hours of cartoons. It was the one time during the week that I got a choice in what I wanted to watch because my dad controlled the remote otherwise. The same goes for YouTube for my daughter; it is her Saturday morning cartoons. There are billions of choices that a child can make on that site, and they can choose to watch it for 30 seconds, 5 minutes, or 1 hour. My older daughter and her friends are constantly on their phones. If you need proof of that, go to any public place where teenagers linger and see how many of them are on their phone while they are hanging out with their friends. Why is this? What is the attraction? Again, it is choice. The teenager can choose to text a friend, watch a social media clip, play a game, or dozens of other activities. They gravitate toward their phone and seem almost addicted, but in reality, they are addicted to the choices that the phone provides.

What if we could tap into this desire of choice? What if we could use this to get students interested and keep them engaged? Heather Wolpert-Gawron (2018) suggested this very thing in her book *Just Ask Us – Kids Speak Out on Student Engagement* when she noted:

According to the student engagement survey, student choice is listed as one of the most engaging strategies a teacher can allow in the classroom. Want to know how to engage students, enthuse them, and bring out their best effort? Want ways to differentiate organically? Give them a voice in their decisions...We have, in our very classrooms, the brains that will solve the problems of tomorrow, but to give them training means we have to give their neurons a chance to solve the problems of to-day. (p. 112)

How can students solve the problems of today if we aren't giving them any choices in what is being taught or how it is being taught? Having choice would certainly do wonders for improving their goal valuation of interest. There are some things that we teach in the classroom that no matter how you deliver it, not matter how much you jazz it up, no matter how excited you get about it, it still isn't very interesting. If we can't make the subject matter interesting, give students other options to peak their interests.

According to Robert Marzano (2001), "When given choice by teachers, students perceive classroom activities as more important. Choice in the classroom has also been linked to increases in student effort, task performance, and subsequent learning" (p. 14, 101). Marzano came to the conclusion that granting students' choice directly aligns with student engagement and motivation and can also help in the goal valuation of importance.

When it comes to the goal valuation of attainable, what better way to convince students they can do it then by letting them determine what "it" looks like. This could be anything from homework to as-sessments. By students setting the bar for themselves, they can see how to attain it because they are the ones who came up with it.

In an effort to practice what I am preaching, I am going to offer you some ways you can offer students more choice in your classroom.

You can pick and choose the ones that work best for you, but remember: the more choice you give students, the more engaged they are going to be, and the more engaged they are, the more they are going to learn.

Seating

So as not to make any sudden moves and scare any of you away like a timid fawn, I'll start with a pretty easy choice that you could start to implement tomorrow: where can students sit in your classroom? By assigning a child where they have to sit, you are taking away their choice the moment they walk into your classroom. I know it is easier to learn their names when they are sitting in the same spot all of the time, but the reality is that if you allow them to sit anywhere they want, most will find a comfortable spot for themselves and then sit there most days.

There are those teachers who do the assigned seating for classroom management purposes. Keeping distracting or rowdy students away from one another makes discipline easier. In general, I would start to get in the habit of making choices in your classroom that aren't about making things easier for you, and instead make decisions based on what is going to be best for kids. I believe that allowing children to pick their own seats is what is best for kids. It gives them some choice and sets to tone for your classroom. Not only that, my classroom in general was pretty fluid, with students switching seats frequently due to groupings or activities.

Let me share a story of how allowing students to choose their seats can actually improve classroom discipline. Just recently, I had the opportunity to teach in China. I was teaching at a camp during their winter break, and my class was composed of 18 Chinese-born fifth graders who spoke decent English. Seven of the boys in my class went to the same school and thus knew each other. When I allowed them to sit wherever they wanted, these boys all sat near one another, and the girls gravitated to tables together as well. Because these boys all knew one another, they horsed around quite a bit. When one boy took things a little too far and proved to be a distraction in class, I moved his seat to one of the tables away from his friends. This kid spent the rest of the day doing everything in his power to prove to me he could behave, so that he could rejoin his friends at their table. At the end of the day, I allowed him to retake his seat under the probation of if he misbehaved again, I would move him back. He was well behaved for the remainder of the camp. The power of the discipline came in that I took away his choice, something all of the other children still had. If I had never given him the choice in the first place, this wouldn't have seemed so bad.

You can do this however you like, but at the beginning of the year, I tell students to sit wherever they like. Wherever they decide to sit is theirs until they prove to me that they cannot sit there. It is a small way to provide student with choice.

Group Members

If you want another easy way to provide students with choice, allow them to choose who they work with in groups when you have collaborative activities. Group work can be difficult for students, especially if there are members who are not pulling their weight. It makes it even tougher if students are stuck with group mates they did not choose. Allowing students to pick their own group members can be done in a few ways:

1. **Let them pick all members:** If you are asking students to work in groups of four, this would mean they would get to decide the people who make up these students. Some teachers avoid this because students will only pick their friends, but in my experience, this gets old, especially if the friend is not a good worker, and the choices start to become about who would be a good group member.

2. **Let them pick a partner and then put two partner groups together:** You might allow students to pick one other person

they really want to work with. Then you get to decide another pair to put them with. This way even though they are working with different people, they had some choice as to who was in their group.

3. **Let them pick who they don't want to work with:** I once saw a teacher do this with her class. She passed out index cards to the students and requested that they write two names of students they really wanted to work with and then one student they did not want to work with. They did not have to explain why they chose who they chose, and the answers were confidential. This way students had some choice in who was *not* in their group.

As teachers, we sometimes want to control who students are working within groups, but we have to understand that they are going to spend the rest of their lives collaborating with others and thus need to learn to work with all sorts of different people. If you don't think the students have chosen a good group or that they will not be effective, that is a lesson they should learn the hard way. It is better to make those bad decisions in school, where it doesn't have a major impact on their life, rather than later down the road when it does.

One time toward the end of the school year, I had a project where students got to collaborate with others. By this time, the class had figured out who the poor group members were; thus, there were four students nobody picked. I figured I would put these four together and they could pull each other down. To my surprise, because there wasn't anyone to pick up their slack, they performed much better than they typically did. In fact, they created one of the best products in the class. But they did learn that because others had a choice, their actions throughout the year took theirs away from them.

Text Choices

One that is also easy to do but might put you out of your comfort zone is allowing students choices in the books they read for a certain unit. There are those educators who become teachers of books, not themes, such as that eighth grade teacher who wants to make sure that every student who passes through her doors reads *The Outsiders* by S.E. Hinton in order to learn about class conflict. What if that is a book that does not appeal to a student, however, or the fact that the book is a bit dated having been published in 1967 means that it does not feel relevant to students? Couldn't the teacher offer a choice of books to deliver the same theme of class conflict? What if she provided five choices:

1. *The Hunger Games* by Suzanne Collins
2. *The Glass Castle* by Jeanette Walls
3. *The Help* by Kathryn Stockett
4. *The Grapes of Wrath* by John Steinbeck
5. *The Hate You Give* by Angie Thomas

This list has a little bit of something for everyone. Books for girls and boys, non-fiction and fiction, classic books, and more recent fare. All students—even reluctant readers—are bound to find something that appeals to them. You could even use audio books—yes, it is reading!—for those students not motivated by actually reading the book. A sixth option could be added where the student chooses for himself. If a boy who is really into graphic novels wants to read *Maus* by Art Spiegelman, as long as he learns the theme you are trying to teach, why wouldn't that work?

Providing them with this choice does a few things. One, for those students who are not real big lovers of reading, it provides them with some motivation because it is a book that has more interest to them. Secondly, it gives them variety. Instead of there being one conversation about the book, there are half a dozen. Because you cannot be in six places at once, the students themselves lead the discussion, and you circulate from group to group, jumping in when you hear something interesting. This is the management part, which I discuss in detail in a later chapter. And third, because they got to choose the book they got to read, instead of you assigning them one, they are more invested in it and thus will read it with more care.

This doesn't have to just be for ELA class. When I was taking social studies classes in college, one of my professors told us we could read a biography about anyone we found interesting. The only caveat was we had to read a second biography on the same person and then compare the differences between the books. I thought this was a fantastic way to teach us about how history can be written and how writer bias can play a part in the shaping of the story. There were 30 different students in the class reading 60 different biographies, but we were all learning the same theme.

You can have students read books in math class. There are many elementary books for kids to choose from where they will be both reading an entertaining story and learning a math concept. Here is a list of a few of these books:

> *The Grapes of Math* by Greg Tang (counting to 10)
>
> *Sir Cumference and All the King's Tens* by Cindy Neuschwander (place value)
>
> *Fraction Fun* by David A. Alder (fractions)
>
> *A Very Improbable Story* by Edward Einhorn (probability)
>
> *What's Your Angle Pythagoras?* by Julie Ellis (geometry and algebra)
>
> *Why Pi?* by Johnny Ball (measurement)

And my personal favorite:

> *Math Curse* by Jon Scieszka and Lane Smith (various math concepts)

A teacher could use this as an end-of-year review, having the students choose one of the books and then teaching others about the math concepts in them.

Book choices are something easy for you to do, and you needn't have read all the books that are choices. You just have to make sure they are teaching the theme you want to get across to students.

Homework

I'm not a big fan of homework. I think many times it is assigned as extra work, rather than because the students need to practice a skill. With that being said, what if you gave students homework, but gave them the option of whether to do it or not?

For example, if you are teaching a high school government class, and you are learning about elections, give students the opportunity to watch the debates if it is a presidential election year or go to the meet the candidates' night to learn about local politicians running for office. Or if you are in an ELA class and are learning about the Romanticism Period, giving students a couple of choices for works they can look up on-line and read. Maybe Poe for the more gothic readers, a short story by Nathaniel Hawthorne for dark romantics, or John Keats for those who prefer poetry. You are challenging students to do the work, but not making it a requirement (and certainly not something you would grade, but you would still offer feedback on).

Homework is a hard thing to motivate students about anyway. Giving them a choice whether to do it or not, as well as choices about the homework itself, creates a that culture of motivation:

> ...when students received a choice of homework they reported higher intrinsic motivation to do homework, felt more competent regarding the homework, and performed better on the unit test compared with when they did not have a choice. In addition, a trend suggested that having choices enhanced homework completion rates compared with when no choices were given. (Patall et al., 2008, p. 281)

It is important to help students see homework not as a chore they have to do, but as an opportunity. It might be an opportunity to learn more about something, or to gain a deeper understanding, or to expand their thinking. Nottingham (2013) recommended the use of homework as a preview activity. If you're doing a unit on Romanticism, the homework could be to look up something you are interested in (fashion, politics, history, art, women's rights) from this period to share with the class. There's still choice, and you are building background knowledge and interest for whatever literature they would be reading. By changing the mindset of homework and looking at it this way, it becomes more about the love of learning, rather than something they have to do.

Resources

If you task students to learn about something, do you need to direct them to specific resources or allow them to find their own? Teach them how to conduct proper research on the Internet, and then let them choose the resources that are best going to help them. This goes a long way in developing independent learners. For example, instead of telling my students they cannot use Wikipedia for any of their sources for a research paper, I taught them what reputable research looks like; this enables them to vet the resource and determine for themselves whether it is reliable.

It doesn't just have to be the Internet. Give students choices about how they can learn about something, whether it be a YouTube video, a personal interview, the reading of an article, or by experiencing it. Students have different learning styles, and they should choose resources that are going to best work with their learning style. A visual learner shouldn't listen to a lecture, and a verbal learner shouldn't read an article. It would work to their strengths if instead the visual learner watched a documentary on the topic or the verbal learner got to have a one-on-one conversation with someone who is an expert on the topic. Allowing them to choose what resources they are going to use will help them to match up the resource with the method in which they learn best, making it more interesting.

Challenge

Since I began as a teacher of gifted students, I was constantly trying to come up with ways to challenge my students beyond what was expected. These students had the potential to go above and beyond, so I designed lessons that allowed them to do this. After a few years, I realized something: strategies used in the gifted classroom are really just good teaching practices in general, and should not be reserved for the gifted, but rather as opportunities for all. I began to use these in my regular classrooms and found that many students welcomed the challenge, while others found the general content challenging enough already. What I started doing was providing students with choices in being challenged.

This could manifest itself in several ways:

- **Bulletin board challenges:** I had a few bulletin boards scattered around the classroom. At these bulletin boards were things such as a trivia question of the week, Sudoku or rebus puzzles, riddles, or other activities meant to stimulate the brain and get kids thinking. Those who were curious had the opportunity to challenge themselves to these while others paid them no mind. The point though was that students had the choice.

- **Book of the month:** This was designed to encourage students to read. I would choose a book I had either read or was reading and would challenge students to do the same. This was not for a class or for a discussion; it was merely an opportunity to read something together for the joy of it.

- **Four corners:** In each of the corners of my room, I had high-interest projects that students could work on if they got their classwork finished. One corner had historical mysteries, another where they could research a career they were interested in, and another allowed them to compare historical movies to what really happened. I would rotate new projects every 9 weeks. These were never a requirement. They were just there for students to explore their curiosity. I was always amazed at how many students chose to do this extra work for the sake of learning something new.

- **Share your expertise:** This invites students to learn about something they have always wanted to learn about and then teach the rest of the class. It is like show and tell on steroids because rather than just showing us something you brought in, you actually have to come up with a lesson so that students can understand it. Through this, the student got to share a passion that motivated them with others, hopefully getting those students interested as well.

- **Outside learning experiences:** I would make students aware of outside learning opportunities that they or their family could attend. This might be a play put on by the local community theatre, an exhibit at the art museum, it might be making them aware of a movie that was currently at the theatres that connects to your content, or sometimes it was classes our parks and recs department or library were offering that they could participate in. The only assessment of this was when students came into class and shared their experiences in my conversations with them.

- **Bonus opportunities:** For projects or lessons, I would present students with the minimum requirements they would need to complete in order to show mastery, but I would also give them choices for ways they could take it above and beyond. For example, in Social Studies class, I had a project where students had to make a list of items in the Renaissance Hall-of-Fame and explain why they chose the items they chose. My bonus opportunity was for them to make a model of what their Hall-of-Fame would look like, using architecture from the Renaissance as an influence. In math class, I would challenge them to find how a certain concept presented itself in the real world, such as shapes in buildings or decimals at the grocery store.

These were all designed with one purpose in mind: to allow students to challenge themselves should they wish to do so. It contributed to the culture of motivation by tapping into the natural curiosity that all children have.

Assessment

Students rarely have any control or say so in the way they are assessed in their learning. Instead, the teacher creates a test they will take, and students are expected to perform well on it. There are a few ways you can provide students with choices when it comes to assessment. It could be:

1. **Form:** Does the assessment even have to be a paper to pencil assessment? What about having choices for different ways to be assessed? One student who is strong at writing might choose to write a response, while another who is skilled at speaking publicly wants to verbalize his answer. You could even provide them with different assessments to choose from. Students could choose the one that best displays their skills or one they would like to learn. The important thing is that they show mastery. It shouldn't matter how they do this.

   Rubric: One of the biggest challenges of allowing students so much choice is that everyone is doing different things. This means one rubric is not going to cover all students. You could have students come up with the benchmarks of what is exemplary work. This could be done as a class together, where you determine what are the criteria for success and what this looks like. Alternatively, you could train students to create their own rubrics. This way, they can create their own personalized rubric, and they are very familiar with the expectations because they are the ones who set them.

Creation/product: Here, students would get to choose a product that best shows their mastery of the learning objectives. They could use a menu board such as this which uses the multiple intelligences:

Figure 5.1 *Product Ideas by Multiple Intelligence*

Naturalist	Visual/Spatial	Body Kinesthetic
- Field Study - Collection - Map	- Collage - Foldable - Board Game	- 3D Model - Play - Hands-On Experiment
Interpersonal	**Student Created**	**Musical Rhythmic**
- Interview - Role play - Teach	- Choose a product that is not on this choice board	- Poem - Perform Song/Rap - Soundtrack
Verbal/ Linguistic	**Intrapersonal**	**Logical/ Mathematical**
- Tri-fold - Brochure - Review	- Journal Entry - Self-Evaluation - Discussion	- Timeline - PowerPoint/ Google Slide - WeVideo/ FlipGrid

Students would get to choose the pathway their learning takes by choosing one of these and then demonstrating what they learned using it.

For further explanation, watch a video tutorial at https://youtu.be/lpDCeC3bCkU.

Finding the Heart of It

In this chapter, I suggested a range of choices you can provide students with in order to improve apathy and motivate students. The design of this chapter is that you shouldn't attempt all of the suggestions contained within, but rather that you would choose which ones you would feel more comfortable making or that would be best for your classroom.

One piece of advice I want to leave you with is that giving over some control in your classroom is probably going to feel unnatural or uncomfortable. I want to remind you that this is a good thing, and the more you do it, the more you will come to find that providing students with choices is more natural than the traditional classroom. Be willing to try and fail—and try and fail some more—until you find the formula that works best for your classroom. There is no one right way to do it.

HOW THE HELL DO WE MOTIVATE THESE KIDS?

Chapter 6

AUTHENTIC LEARNING

"Dear High School, instead of useless math formulas and Freudian English analyses, you should have taught me about taxes, résumés, and cover letters. I'm not ready for the real world."
- Anonymous post on Pinterest

What is the purpose of school? There are many different philosophies and ideas about why students go to school and what is supposed to happen after they leave. My own philosophy is that school is a part of the component of learning how to survive and thrive in the real world. Your parents provide you with certain aspects, such as feeding you, putting a roof over your head, and providing clothing until you can do those things on your own. Your friends influence you, especially in the teenage years, where they help to shape your likes and dislikes, your social circles, and part of your outlook of the world. School provides the basic reading, writing, and arithmetic that will be needed to function in the real world once school is over. The idea is that students leave high school being prepared to take on what might come their way, whether it be college, a career, or making life decisions with impunity.

When I was teaching third graders, I realized that my expectations were not that they could leave the elementary school and go get themselves a competitive job in an industry they desired. My main goal was to get them ready for the next grade, as well as looking down the road a little further to provide them with something that would help them be successful in school and life. This might be a 21st century skill such as how to conduct proper research, giving a competent persuasive speech, or learning to work well with others to produce something together that you could not have done individually.

The problem with some schooling is that many times, it is taught in a vacuum. The way we set things up, whether it be teaching subjects separate from one another that would otherwise go together or breaking something down so much that students cannot see how it goes back together, doesn't show the big picture. Often, students are not even aware why they should be learning something. Part of the solution is what I talked about in Chapter Four; in visible learning, it is transparent to students *what* they are learning, *why* they are learning it, and *how* they will use this in the future. By doing this, students are taken out of the vacuum and can see how all of these thousands of puzzle pieces they are learning about daily will somehow all fit together into one complete picture that represents their life as an adult.

Another part of the solution is making it abundantly clear how the lesson they are learning manifests itself in the real world. It is about making the learning authentic, enabling students to see how they will use this when they are an adult. This is the *why* of learning. There are many things you can do in your classroom to make the learning have a real-world application and as a result, be more authentic. But it is not just about bringing someone from the outside into the classroom or taking students on field trips or giving them VR goggles so they can experience a whole different world. It's about having an authentic classroom in which students are consistently exposed to real-world problems that they have to figure out how to solve. By doing so, they will understand how to solve them when they are front and center in their own lives.

There are many strategies that could be used to bring authentic learning to students, but the four I am going to discuss in this chapter are commensurate with motivation. These act as a structure in which you can put all the elements of a culture of motivation into your classroom from the caring, visible learning, choice, and reflection. You will use effective management in order to run your authentic classroom, but we will talk much more about that in the next chapter. The strategies that I suggest in this chapter are inquiry learning, project-based learning, problem-based learning, and case-based learning.

Inquiry Learning

Inquiry learning is the umbrella under which the other three teaching strategies fall. All three use the idea of inquiry learning in one way or another, they just offer you options for different ways to deliver this to students. Just as I provide students with choices so that they may find how to best use their strengths and interests, I try to provide the same to teachers I am working with on professional development. We all know there is no one correct way to teach, otherwise everyone would simply be doing that. There are, however, various strategies that best fit into the style you bring to the classroom. Out of these three strategies that employ inquiry learning, hopefully you will find one that best suits your needs.

Inquiry-based learning (IBL) is a teaching strategy where instead of the teacher presenting information to students, there is a question, problem, or scenario posed for students to consider. Sometimes this is provided by the teacher; in more enlightened classrooms, these are generated by the students. Here is where IBL becomes very different from the traditional method of teaching. Instead of the teacher commanding the classroom and leading students where they need to go, students allow their curiosity and their questions to drive where the learning will take them. Students identify and research items in order to come up with a solution, expanding their knowledge naturally. What they are learning is what they have discovered, not what the teacher has given them, making it intrinsic. The learning is student-centered and active, meaning that students will be engaged; as a result of this engagement, they will be more motivated.

This notion might seem very uncomfortable to a teacher in today's classroom, with the Common Core Standards that need to be taught and the tests that hold her accountable for what students learn. The argument becomes, "We do not have time to let students wander around, pursuing dead-ends." They argue, "We have to keep these kids on task, so we are covering all of the standards we need to." Of course, the reality is inquiry-based learning reinforces curriculum content because the lessons learned from IBL are enduring. Because it is based on the curiosity of the student, this sparks the brain to remember better because they have achieved metacognition. This is when students connect what they are learning to their own lives and thus provide context for why it is important for them to learn it. In a traditional classroom, where the strategy for the student will be to memorize a content standard for the test, he is not going to be able to recall it later. Instead of worrying about wasting class time, make sure you are using what class time you have more efficiently. You'll be amazed at how much more effective your lessons will be if students can remember what they learned before.

IBL follows a particular cycle, which is illustrated in the figure below.

Figure 6.1 *Inquiry-Based Learning Cycle*

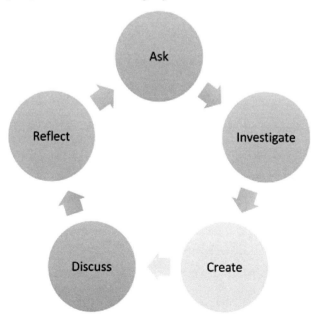

HOW THE HELL DO WE MOTIVATE THESE KIDS?

The descriptions of each are:

> **Ask:** Using prior knowledge and understanding, students pose an essential question or questions concerning a given topic.
>
> **Investigate:** Students then collect evidence to either prove or disprove the essential question.
>
> **Create:** From this information, students create new knowledge and understanding.
>
> **Discuss:** Students present, discuss, and debate their results.
>
> **Reflect:** The metacognition of thinking about what the student learned from the activity.

As you can see, using this IBL framework allows all of the other steps in motivation to be employed. By asking questions students are making their learning visible, by providing them with choice it increases interest, and by having the investigation be about something authentic, there is certainly a real-world application.

You will also be able to teach the content standards you are responsible for, while simultaneously teaching students valuable 21st century skills that result from using IBL. Some of the advantages of IBL are:

- Nurtures student passion and talents
- Empowers student voice and honor student choice
- Teaches grit, perseverance, and self-direction
- Develops strong research skills
- Trains student to ask questions in seeking to understand
- Fosters curiosity and a love of learning
- Solves real-world problems (MacKenzie, 2017)

Sounds like this is the perfect structure to foster students' love of learning.

Problem-Based Learning

We do a lot of problem-solving in our lives. Whether it is figuring out how to get into a parking spot, getting the television remote control to work properly, or determining just how much chocolate cake you can eat before making yourself sick, we try and determine the best way to solve these problems. Sometimes we are successful at these tasks, and get into the parking spot or get the television on the channel we want to watch. Other times, it is a massive fail, and you end up regretting having that final piece of cake and wishing that your stomach would stop hurting. While these may seem like small issues, these are problems we encounter on a daily basis, and the better we are at figuring out how to solve them, the more often we are going to make successful decisions. It is especially important to get good at problem-solving when larger-scale, possibly life-changing issues arise and we have to figure out how to traverse these. If you are determining whether you can afford to buy a house, these are several factors to consider such as:

- How far is the location of the house as compared to where you work?
- What school system does the house reside in?
- Does the house have room for more if you are starting a family?
- What is the layout of the house?
- How quickly can you move in?
- Is it a new or used house, and which is better?
- What is the neighborhood like?
- How much will it cost?
- Is your credit good enough to get a loan?
- Do you see yourself staying there long-term?

During this process of problem-solving, you may come to the conclusion that you need to obtain additional information that you do not possess in order to solve it. This is a recognition of a need to learn. This is what problem-based learning is.

For the house buying scenario, you might have to find out what your credit score is, have a long conversation with your spouse about where you see yourselves in 10 years, determine whether you plan to have children, and figure out whether you are ready for such an investment. This need to learn in order to solve the problem is the heart of problem-based learning. The better students get at it, the better decisions they are going to make in their own lives.

The basic structure of problem-based learning (PrBL), as compared to traditional learning, looks like this:

Figure 6.2 *Problem-Based Learning Process*

Traditional learning usually follows this process:

The process of problem-based learning:

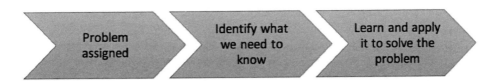

In the traditional learning process, the teacher is the one who is in control. He tells the students what they need to know, and assigns a problem so that students can apply what they have learned. It is very much a teacher-centered model. In contrast, problem-based learning starts with the problem, which can be assigned by the teacher or developed by the students. Then the students must identify what they need to know and how they will gather these resources. They are also the ones who decide how they will apply what they have learned to solve the problem. It is very student-centered, with the main role of the teacher making the problem as authentic as possible.

This means replacing math problems in the form of story problems about people and situations we do not know with real-life problems. When learning about rate problems, instead of assigning a question such as the following...

> Jerry types 2/3 of a page in ½ an hour. How much can she type in 1 hour?

...give students problems that they would see in the real world, such as determining the unit price of milk at the grocery store:

> Which one is the better buy?
>
> - 2 liters of Milk at $3.80
> - 1.5 liters of Milk at $2.70

This is something that would be of more use in everyday life. How important would it be in life to be able to compare prices and determine which one is better? It would certainly save you money.

You can look at larger problems as well. If students are learning about persuasive writing, rather than having them do a literary essay that will be seen by no one but the teacher, have students identify a cause they would like to influence and then figure out who to send letters or emails to in order to have an impact. Let's say that students decide they want to change the curfew laws in the town they live in because teens driving home from work can get pulled over. Students would identify who to best write these letters to whether it be a local councilperson, a letter to the editor, or to the police department. Students are still learning the skill of persuasive writing, but they are more motivated to do a good job because their work will potentially have influence. This is the power of problem-based learning when it is done in an authentic manner.

If you are willing to try problem-based learning, here is a structure that can be used when developing lessons for it:

1. Present the problem.

2. List what is known.

3. Develop a problem statement.

4. List what is needed.

5. List actions, solutions, or hypothesis.

6. Present and support the solution.

The best part is that you as the teacher only need to provide the first step. Then, it is up to the students to develop the rest. You are just managing the classroom and providing resources, something that we will discuss further in the next chapter on effective management.

Here is what this would look if you were creating a problem-based learning example for a teacher:

> A teacher has 30 students in his classroom. He is teaching a unit on the importance of how to research.

Constraints

- Have 1 week to get the lesson in

- Lesson must be engaging

- Should be choice in the lesson

- Have to assess mastery somehow

- Plan this lesson.

Notice the simplicity of the problem that is provided; it states the problem, lists the constraints, and provides a final product to display mastery. The ideas are provided by the people working on the problem.

For further explanation, watch a video tutorial at
https://youtu.be/KA1ct609-xg.

Project-Based Learning

Project-based learning (PBL) is another strategy that follows the inquiry-based model. Although there is a lot of overlap, the major difference between problem and project-based is that PrBL starts with the problem and works forward from there. Project-based learning starts at the end and then works its way backward.

Figure 6.3 *Project-Based Learning Process*

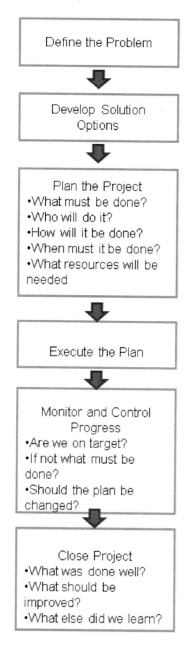

When my students were learning about causes of the Civil War, I asked them to create a podcast about one of the possible causes. It had to be 10 minutes long, and could only be audio. The point of my choosing this particular product was twofold; I thought that students knowing how to make a podcast would be valuable, given that they were starting to become popular. It was a skill that would benefit them long after they forgot what they had learned about a group of people who existed over 5,000 years ago. The second thing I wanted students to get was to find a way to explain themselves in words only. There would be no visuals to which they could refer, and they had to explain themselves with enough detail and use enough examples so that people listening understood what they were talking about. Finally, the students learned about the causes of the Civil War, a standard I was required to cover as part of my curriculum. Even though I did not give them a choice on the product they had to create, they did have a choice of their topic. This way students could find something interesting they wanted to learn more about and then describe what they had learned to others through the podcast. We then jigsawed these podcasts together, listening to them and getting a good picture of what events led to the Civil War.

There are many different structures to project-based learning but rather than use one developed by educators, I turned to the business world. These are the steps that project managers use when overseeing a project. My thought was that if I want to get students ready for the real world, I should expose them to these, as they might see them again once they start their careers.

As you can see with the steps listed here, the process starts with the problem. It is typically a content standard that needs to be taught to students. Most of my work as the teacher came in developing the solution options, which is just a fancy business term for what product will students produce to show me they got it. What this looked like was students were either given a product they needed to produce or even better, given a choice for how to show what they learned.

Whichever one it was, I tried to find ways to make it relevant to their lives or had real-world connections. When we were learning about economics, students had to create a product with a business plan and present it to a panel of local business owners à la Shark Tank. When students learned about world religions, one of the product requirements was they had to interview someone from that religion, but how they decided to present their information to the class was their choice with some students doing the traditional PowerPoint, some creating a website, while others making a pamphlet. For westward expansion, students had to write a research paper using MLA formatting, but they could choose any topic they wanted to as long as it was related to westward expansion and had enough research to support a paper. The point is that instead of starting with the problem that was pushing them forward, it was an end product that was pulling them along.

It is important to provide students with choice in their products. I learned very quickly that my students were often smarter than me and almost always more creative. I learned this valuable lesson from Wesley, a sixth grader I had in my science class. He was a bright child, but not terribly motivated. He turned in average work at best, although I knew he could produce much better if he tried a little harder. When we were learning about physical and chemical changes, I gave students a choice of 10 different products they could produce to show me they had mastered the idea of this scientific principle. Wesley looked at the list and said,

"Mr. Stanley. I don't like any of these."

I looked at Wesley and knew that if I made him do one of the 10 I had chosen, he would turn in average work. I figured, what did I have to lose?

"What would you like to do?"

"I want to create a video game that teaches the differences between physical and chemical change."

And that's what he did. His video game involved a knight on a quest. He would come to a tree that was blocking his path and have to use his sword to chop through it. The player had to indicate whether this was a physical or chemical change. Then the knight would come to a gate that was rusted shut and have to identify which change this was. It went on and on, and I was amazed at Wesley's product. From that moment on, I tried as much as possible to provide latitude in the products students did and see what they could come up with. This choice went a long way in taking a topic that was not that exciting to them and making the learning engaging because they were working on a product of their desire.

Here is what this would look if you were creating a project-based learning example for a teacher:

Planning a Project

Using the materials provided you will have 30 minutes to create the basic outline of a project.

You will follow the first three steps of a project, defining the problem, developing service options, and planning the project.

You can use the content standards provided or provide one of your own.

Step #1: Define the Problem

This problem can typically be a specific content standard.

Choose one of the following to work with:

CCSS.MATH.CONTENT.7.SP.A.1

Use random sampling to draw inferences about a population.

CCSS.ELA-LITERACY.RI.8.7

Evaluate the advantages and disadvantages of using different mediums (e.g., print or digital text, video, multimedia) to present a particular topic or idea.

MS-PS3-4 Energy

Plan an investigation to determine the relationships among the energy transferred, the type of matter, the mass, and the change in the average kinetic energy of the particles, as measured by the temperature of the sample.

Step #2: Develop Solution Options

This is basically deciding what the product will be for the project. What will students create/produce that displays the skills you want to measure?

Essential Question: What product would demonstrate the mastery I want students to be able to achieve?

Step #3: Plan the Project

Using a blank calendar, plan the basic activities by working backwards from the end product.

Everything revolves around the solution options or product that shows mastery. The more choice you give to students in these solution options, the most buy-in they will have, and the more motivated they will be to learn.

> **For further explanation, watch a video tutorial at**
> **https://youtu.be/lr_clQhXuKY.**

Case-Based Learning

Case-based learning (CBL) is the lesser known of these strategies but has been used for many years in the medical and law fields. Case-based learning has the teacher provide the central resource(s) that will be the center of the learning. As its name implies, this is typically a real-life case that students are being asked to solve or improve. Case-based learning is centered around learning from the past in order to inform decisions in the future.

The source could be small and is meant to spark the ideas, or it could be an entire book. For example, if you are teaching a lesson about racism, you could use a statement from the Conagra Food Brand and its depiction of Mrs. Butterworth on its syrup bottle:

> The Mrs. Butterworth's brand, including its syrup packaging, is intended to evoke the images of a loving grandmother. We stand in solidarity with our Black and Brown communities and we can see that our packaging may be interpreted in a way that is wholly inconsistent with our values.
>
> We understand that our actions help play an important role in eliminating racial bias and as a result, we have begun a complete brand and packaging review on Mrs. Butterworth's.
>
> It's heartbreaking and unacceptable that racism and racial injustices exist around the world. We will be part of the solution. Let's work together to progress toward change. (Conagra Brands, 2020, para. 1-3)

This could be the impetus for students creating a logo that would evoke the values of equality.

Or, a teacher could use the book *Getting Away with Murder: The True Story of the Emmett Till Case*. This is a non-fiction book by Chris Crowe chronicling the case of a young Black boy who was kidnaped and murdered for allegedly whistling at a White woman in Mississippi in 1955. This book could be used to develop a case, whether it be a mock trial or creating a journal with entries from different people in the case and their perspectives.

The steps to case-based learning look like this:

Figure 6.4 *Case-Based Learning Cycle*

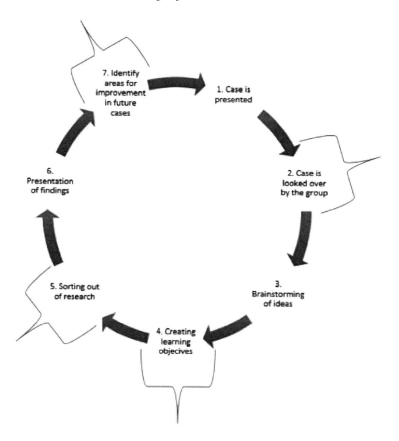

Even though the teacher is the one who gives the students the primary resource, just like the other inquiry models discussed in this chapter, the learning is student-driven, and thus student-centered. The students look over the resource, brainstorm ideas of where they can take it, create learning objectives, sort out the research, present whatever conclusion they come to, and of course, reflect on their learning.

In the graphic depicting the cycle of case-based learning steps, you will notice the brackets for Steps 2, 4, 5, and 7. These are the places where the teacher can be the 'meddler in the middle.' While observing students working, the teacher can approach and ask questions designed to get them to pause and think. It will also allow the teacher to have conversations with students to continue to develop that caring environment.

Here is an example of case-based learning for a teacher:

> Tom is an eighth-grade teacher who decides for his lesson on rocks and minerals, he is going to have the students work in groups. He puts them into groups of 5 students and does this alphabetically until he has 6 groups.
>
> He decides he is going to have them research different types of rocks and minerals and to learn the three types: metamorphic, igneous, and sedimentary. After a couple of days of researching, Tom gets the following email.
>
> Mr. Thomas, my son is not getting along with his group.
>
> After researching, each group must create a poster that defines the three different types of rocks and minerals. Each group is provided with a piece of posterboard and a package of markers.
>
> A couple of days into this, Tom gets a phone call from another parent. The gist of the conversation is that this parent's daughter is complaining that she is having to do all of the work and that there are members of her group who are not doing anything.
>
> Finally, there is a presentation aspect where students have to find an example of a metamorphic, igneous, and sedimentary rock around their neighborhood and explain how they know which type of rock or mineral it is. For one of the presentations, the group has an igneous example and a metamorphic one, but when prompted for the sedimentary, one of the group members shrugs his shoulders and Tom marks the rubric accordingly.
>
> The lesson is graded using a rubric. Tom checks the appropriate boxes, tallies a holistic letter grade, and gives it back to the group before moving on to the next lesson.

Analyze this case and determine several strategies that could be used to make this lesson better.

To some, case-based learning might seem more appropriate for high school students, but I used it with my elementary students. When we were learning about laws and how the court system works, we put Goldilocks on trial for breaking and entering, using the children's story to pull our evidence and eyewitness accounts from. When looking at history with my middle schoolers, I tried as much as possible to expose students to primary documents and to use these to draw conclusions for themselves, such as when we used the Federalist and Anti-Federalist Papers to argue our own Constitutional Convention. Case-based learning is great for science because you can look at actual science experiments or innovations and consider whether things could have been done differently.

> **For further explanation, watch a video tutorial at https://youtu.be/vEIdAVLIBl0.**

Finding the Heart of It

All of these inquiry strategies are great for making learning authentic. For problem-based learning, simply base the problem on an issue affecting the world or their community. In project-based learning, make sure the product uses a skill that students might need later in their lives. Case-based learning typically uses a real-life case for which students try to develop a solution. It is these authentic learning experiences that make the learning relevant to a student and it is this relevance that causes them to be more engaged and thus more motivated.

If we don't want students to play the game of school and instead, learn for learning's sake, it is necessary to offer strategies in our classrooms that are more student-centered, that personalize the learning, offers choices, and shows them the relevance of what they are learning.

Problem-, project-, and case-based learning are three such strategies.

You don't have to choose just one of these. You can choose the one that works best for you or that you are the most comfortable with and try that first. Once you get your feet a little wet, then you can branch out and try others. To liven things up and keep students on their toes, I like to offer a variety of these strategies, using problem-based learning when learning about cells, project-based learning when becoming an expert on a topic of choice concerning mathematics, and case-based learning when looking at the Civil War and the trial of Dred Scott. Some strategies work better with certain topics, so mix and match as best you can. When in doubt, choose the one that you feel is best going to provide your students with a chance to learn on their terms.

Even if you don't choose one of these inquiry strategies, you must pick a teaching method that allows student learning to be personalized. Traditional methods usually don't allow for this to occur, so you might have to learn something new outside of your comfort zone. The good news is that by doing this, you will know exactly how your students will feel in your class.

HOW THE HELL DO WE MOTIVATE THESE KIDS?

Chapter 7

EFFECTIVE MANAGEMENT

"There are only two ways in which a manager can impact an employee's output: motivation and training. If you are not training, then you are basically neglecting half the job."
- Andy Grove

When you read the above quote, you might be wondering why I am using it in a book about motivating students in the classroom. After all, students are not employees... are they? They spend as much time doing school as many adults do work, and there's even work to be done after school. I'm not saying you should treat your students like an employee. What I am trying to do is shift your mindset a little. If you frame the education of students as on-the-job training for life, your actions and lessons become more pertinent. You are not just getting students ready for the next grade, you are providing them with skills and training that is hopefully going to prepare them for life. This is why you aim your lessons towards the goal; this is why you provide them with a range of choices; and it is certainly why you provide them with as many authentic experiences as possible, all while you are showing them that you care.

I also want to shift your mindset on what the role of the teacher is in a classroom where the strategies talked about in the authentic learning chapter come to life. If you are using these strategies, the delivery of the learning goes from the teacher to the student. It is not the teacher leading the learning. It is the students figuring out how to learn with some guidance from the teacher. Because of this, the role becomes more a 'guide from the side' rather than a 'sage from the stage.' This new role means you are going to organize your classroom differently. This chapter will provide you with some sound advice for what this may look like.

Because this will seem unfamiliar to students as well, you might have to do some training to get them used to this. This also applies to skills such as note taking, research, and studying. In managing your classroom, these are all things that need to be considered for training.

Face Time

This simply refers to how much time are you the teacher spending in front of the classroom. In a traditional classroom where you are the deliverer of the information, you would need to be in front of the classroom a lot because students need to be able to hear and see you. In a classroom that is student-led, this face time diminishes considerably because the students are the ones whose voices need to be heard and students are the ones driving their learning.

Sometimes this means you have to check yourself before you wreck yourself (or your students' class time). I struggled with this at first when I had transformed the focus of my classroom into a project-based learning. The basic structure of class was students were either given or developed a project, and then they were given time in class to work on solving this project or developing a product to show mastery. My involvement included me going around and having conversations with students about where their projects were and helping aim them better if they got off course. Occasionally, though, I would revert to old habits.

One day, I told students that I just needed their attention for the beginning of class, so that I could give them some guidance in the project they were currently working on. I went over something with them, and when I finished talking, a student raised his hand. "Mr. Stanley, you've only given us 15 minutes of class time to work on our projects."

Low and behold, I glanced at the clock to notice that I had indeed sucked a good half hour of their class time away from them, and wasn't giving them the time and space to work on what they needed to. I didn't even realize I had been talking so long! I think this is something that happens to a lot of teachers. We are so used to commanding the room that we are not aware when we are bogarting the microphone.

After this incident, I instituted the 10-minute rule in my classroom. I bought an egg timer that had a magnet so it could be affixed to the white board. When I needed to make an announcement to students or give them some direct instruction, I set the timer for 10 minutes. During this time, students were to give me their undivided attention. In return, I would stop talking once the timer went off, leaving them with more time to work in class.

> **For further explanation, watch a video tutorial at https://youtu.be/qVHVDR5PGnM.**

It doesn't have to be this extreme, but the thing I learned by managing my face time within that 10 minutes was to pick my words carefully and get to the point a lot quicker. It made me more efficient as a teacher and clearer in the visible learning of my lessons. Some teachers do not need such a structure in order to do this, but for me, it was rather helpful.

No matter what strategy you choose, make sure to watch your face time and save your thoughts and insights about the project to use in your individual conversations you will have with students—which, by the way, will help develop the caring aspect. You will be able to offer advice that is specific to that student and his or her situation, thereby personalizing the learning. Students will be more engaged in these conversations than if you were lecturing to the class.

Resources

One of the major roles for teachers is to provide resources for their students. In a traditional classroom, resources take the form of the information and content that you provide for them. In an inquiry classroom, the resources shift to ones that students can use, not ones they merely receive. Instead of providing students with an article about the Big Bang Theory, you provide them with a laptop that can be used to research various theories. Instead of showing them how the Pythagorean theorem works, you might provide them a link to a YouTube video that does a really good job of demonstrating it. Rather than having them read about an immigrant's experience, allow them to use their phone to call someone who is not a native of this country and get their firsthand perspective on what it is like to be an immigrant.

In the 21st century classroom, where most students have their own computer with Internet access, we need to understand as educators that by going and getting the information for them, we are teaching them content but not how to learn. Giving them the opportunity to find information for themselves is teaching them to learn. It is giving them real-world skills.

If you are employing the authentic learning strategies discussed previously, your resources might include:

- Computers/Internet access
- Phone/Zoom
- Online educational programs that challenge students
- Directory for local university and its departments
- Consumables such as paper, poster board, and other such things to create their products
- Markers, pencils, pens
- Scissors, glue,
- Rulers of various sorts

- Space to work
- Suggestions for folks to network with

You should essentially consider your authentic learning classroom to be organized with any tools that students would need to demonstrate authentic mastery of what they are learning.

Skills Training

There will still be some instances in which you will need to provide direct instruction. One of these times would be in teaching skills that would be helpful in students' quest for learning. You can tell a student to research, but do they really know how to research? You can tell them to study for a test, but have they developed study skills that enable them to learn the material rather than just memorize it? If you were to give your students 3 weeks to work on a project, would they spend that time developing their best work, or would they wait until the last second to try and complete it? Sometimes we assume—especially with older students—that they already possess these skills through years of schooling. Many times, what students have developed are bad habits. Identifying skills that individual students seem to lack and helping them to learn these is going to make your students' better learners.

Some skills you might want to consider focusing on would be:
- Public speaking
- Study skills
- Note-taking
- Organization
- Task prioritization
- Leadership
- Critical thinking/problem-solving
- Technology literacy

- Written communication
- Adaptability

There are many different ways you can teach these skills, from giving students opportunities to use them, to having exercises where they develop them, to sitting down with them and showing them step by step.

Don't think you should do these skills only at a certain age. I have taught third graders note-taking skills. I have had to teach seniors in high school how to write a thesis statement. Students are capable of learning these skills at an early age, and they are capable of a refresher when they are older. To this very day, at the age of 48 years old, I am still learning things when it comes to public speaking, even after delivering thousands of presentations. There is always room to learn and refine your skills.

Group Work

One of the skills I left off my list was the skill of collaborating with others. I did not include it because it is important enough to merit its own section. The reason for its importance is that you will be tasked with working with others for the rest of your life, whether it be family, co-workers, teammates, or friends. It is an important skill to possess for success in the real world, and is highly valued by employers.

In schools, however, we do not do a good job of deliberately teaching this skill to students. We put students in groups and tell them to produce something without giving them the tools to be able to work effectively, then we are surprised when they begin to hate group work. The reason for their hatred is not that they do not like working with others, it stems from the fact that they have never been provided with examples of what successful collaboration looks like or coping mechanisms for dealing with issues.

A few things to consider when organizing students into groups that will allow them to be more effective and to learn collaboration skills:

- **Creating group norms:** This involves the group setting guidelines for what is and what is not acceptable. It is providing the expectations for group members so that they know how to behave and act in their group

> **For further explanation, watch a video tutorial at https://youtu.be/JzQo7Pt8mBw.**

- **Roles:** Having specific roles for students in the group and holding them accountable for that role goes a long way in combating the biggest gripe about working in groups which is that things aren't fair. What often happens is one person doesn't do what he is supposed to and the entire group gets penalized as a result. These roles can be identified by the students or the teacher can suggest some roles. I always did a group skills inventory with students at the beginning of the school year. This provided me with an idea of what they thought they were good at, enabling me to group them according to these skills.

> **For further explanation, watch a video tutorial at https://youtu.be/VxYx0Dzqios.**

- **Having coping strategies:** When something goes wrong in a group, many times the students turn to the teacher to solve these problems. Unfortunately, in the real world, there will not be a teacher there to help them, so it is important for students to learn how to solve these problems themselves. I provide them with a troubleshooting sheet to figure out such issues:
  - Figuring out how to get started
  - Not meeting the deadline or objectives of the lesson provided

- Disagreements between team members
- Getting off task

I then give them the space to figure out any problems as a group rather than me stepping in and doing it for them.

- **Choosing of groups:** There are many ways to form groups. Some of these are:
  - Teacher choice
  - Student choice
  - Combination of the two
  - Strength based
  - Interest based
  - Skill based

I have always found a combination of these to work best.

> **For further explanation, watch a video tutorial at https://youtu.be/BvOB1cStL8o.**

- **Self/peer evaluations:** Having the students evaluate one another and the effectiveness in working with others allows them to hold each other accountable rather than leaving the teacher with all of the oversight. Students use the norms to determine whether a person has been an asset to the group or has simply been an ass. This takes the disciplining yoke off of your back and allows the students to police themselves, much like they will have to do when working in a group in the real world. This should be factored into the student's overall assessment so that it has some weight to it.

> **For further explanation, watch a video tutorial at https://youtu.be/x1VzZrNt7tU.**

Managing

All of this is well and good, but what does the teacher do while the kids are working? Should you catch up on correspondence, or maybe read that book that has been gathering dust on your bookshelf? The role of the teacher is more of a project manager in the business world. A project manager does not actually do the work or execute the actions. They oversee those that are doing these tasks and aim them in the direction they need to go, while leaving them alone to do the work they need to do. This balancing act is the role you will play in the classroom.

Some strategies for managing students successfully are:

- **Managing stress:** Your students will probably not have been exposed to this way of learning in their past schooling. When you have been spoon-fed your learning your entire school career, it is difficult to suddenly have to do it for yourself. It is like a zoo animal who has had a keeper deliver three square meals a day being thrust out into the wilderness to fend for themselves. It has to be a gradual release, and it is your job as the teacher to help them adjust. When you see a student begin to get frustrated, have a conversation with her about options that she can troubleshoot. When a student seems to have bitten off more than he can chew, gently aim him back on track with some encouraging words or suggestions.

- **Giving students space:** As learners, we tend to do the best, more effective learning when we are allowed to go big and to make mistakes. In fact, being pushed to the brink of failure causes a lot of people to be very innovative and come up with things they would not have had they had it easier or more resources. Kids come by this naturally. Think about how many times a child fell while trying to walk, but got right back up and tried again. Could you imagine if that child simply folded his arms and said, "Nah. I'm not going to try to walk anymore"? You see this mostly in the playing of video games. A kid will try hundreds of times to defeat a level, failing time and time again, and yet persevering. Your classroom needs to be a place where students feel they can take risks and not have their grades or their status tarnished as a result. By going around and having conversations with students you are conducting a formative assessment where you are guiding them on the correct track. Very rarely will they be able to fail when they are being assessed for mastery. They will have made mistakes along the way, which is perfectly alright. With your guidance from the side, they will learn from these mistakes.

> **For further explanation, watch a video tutorial at https://youtu.be/BCNcJTNldDY.**

- **Keeping their eyes on the prize:** There are various ways to do this, but what has worked in my classroom are graphic organizers to help remind them of what they are trying to achieve. These come in three forms:
  - **Student contract/syllabus:** This usually contains their essential question or learning objectives for quick reference. This is part of the clarity of learning in that when you introduce the lesson you either go over the syllabus or to have more involvement or buy-in, have them create their own learning contract. Then you occasionally pull those out and make sure they go over what their main learning goal is, comparing it to the work they have been doing. This of course is in addition to having this learning target on the board, your class website, and other places.

> **For further explanation, watch a video tutorial at https://youtu.be/wfEoekY7bc0.**

- **Calendar:** This can either be provided by the teachers as a guideline for the students—or, better yet, you can let them organize their own calendar and what will be done by when. This involves prioritizing, organizing, and managing their time. When I come around to talk to them, I have them pull out the calendar and see where their progress is; if they are way off, we develop a plan for getting back on track

> **For further explanation, watch a video tutorial at https://youtu.be/z8FHraHxKDU.**

- **Rubric:** This is either teacher-provided, class-created, or student-developed. Whichever, the rubric acts as the blueprint for building an excellent product. Students can simply follow this and it makes clear what the expectations are. The key, though, is having a rubric that shows students what this looks like with descriptive language and clarity, rather than vague statements such as "does a great job." What does a "great job" look like? What actions does this entail? How does one accomplish this "great job"? A well-written rubric goes a long way in making it clear to students what they are supposed to be doing and how they can do this with quality.

> **For further explanation, watch a video tutorial at https://youtu.be/H_eGyATb4JA.**

Conferences

Yet another strategy for effective management is to conference with students periodically. Because you are no longer stuck at the front of the class, you have the freedom to move about and talk with students and/or groups. The basic purpose of these meetings is to see where students are in the learning process, determine whether they need any resources or instruction to get them where they need to be, and then leave them alone to do their work. This independent work is where the learning takes place.

There are three different kinds of conferences I typically have with students:

- **Status reviews:** These are basically maintenance reviews, checking in with individuals or a group and making sure they are where they need to be in regard to the calendar and deadlines. This involves the teacher and students sitting down with the calendar and seeing where exactly the group is.

- **Reflection/process reviews:** These ask students to reflect on their learning thus far. You might ask them questions such as, "What have you done well?" or "What do we want to improve for the future?" The idea is that students are reflecting as they are going along, which is an important part of the learning process.

- **Design reviews:** When students are getting to the point where they are creating their product that shows mastery, this is making sure it shows the mastery that students intend it to. It is looking not only at the quality of the product, but whether the student conveyed what the learning objective was, thus making the learning visible for others.

These conferences are also the perfect place to build relationships with students. You will learn more about what and how students are learning in these 5-minute conversations than from any work they might turn in.

I usually provide students with a blank calendar whenever working on one of the inquiry-based learning assignments, and we schedule conferences so students know when they are happening and can be prepared. There are also the impromptu meetings where I see a student struggling, or something really interesting a student is working on, or have generally become bored and just want to have a conversation with someone. You don't want to have too many of these, because you don't want to seem like you are micromanaging students, but they go a long way in showing that you care.

Finding the Heart of It

If you expect students to learn a different way, you have to be willing to teach a different way. Teaching in this manner can be very uncomfortable for teachers because they often feel like they are not in control of the classroom. Let me let you in on a little secret: in a student-centered classroom, you are not in control—they are. This is what makes it engaging and provides motivation. Just because you are not in control though does not mean you are not managing the classroom. Use this opportunity to get to know your students better and show them the caring side of you. Take advantage of the fact that you do not have to be commanding the classroom the entire period. That is exhausting. Sit back and enjoy yourself as you watch your students learn for themselves. As teachers, we are often so busy running the classroom that we cannot observe individual students. This allows you to do that. Although uncomfortable at first, the rewards far outweigh any risks.

HOW THE HELL DO WE MOTIVATE THESE KIDS?

Chapter 8

REFLECTION

"Research...demonstrated that employees who spent 15 minutes at the end of the day reflecting about lessons learned, performed 23% better after 10 days than those who did not reflect."
- Harvard Business Review

Most people know that reflection makes learning much more powerful. This is not a secret, but it can be a lot like flossing your teeth. No matter how good you know it is for you, you never take the time to do it because you want to get on to other things. We need to take the time to have students reflect on their learning. This simple action reinforces what they have learned and makes it more enduring. Like flossing, it can be a pain in the rear, but we know that by doing it, we will benefit in the long run.

For years, the way I ran my classroom was as follows: I introduced a project, students worked on it producing a product to show mastery, I graded this, and we moved on to the next project. I was certainly getting a good idea of what content and skills students were learning, but I was not getting the picture of what they truly were learning. Students have a funny way of learning what they want from a lesson. You can have all of the visible learning you want, but much like the proverbial horse, they can choose to drink the water, bathe in it, or stick their nose in it and blow bubbles.

Once I understood this, I came to the realization I needed a way to capture what it was students were truly learning from my projects. That was when I introduced reflection at the end of every project. This came in various forms, but the structure was nearly always the same:

1. **Retrospection:** thinking back about a situation or experience.
2. **Self-evaluation:** critically analyzing and evaluating the actions and feelings associated with the experience.
3. **Reorientation:** using the results of self-evaluation to influence future approaches to similar situations or experiences. (Quinn, 2000)

No matter which form it took, I wanted to make sure students were being thoughtful about the reflection they were doing. I was not looking for canned answers, or ones that were designed to stroke my ego. I wanted to know what students really got from it—warts and all. In fact, the more warts the better, because we can learn from these warts. This meant if the student reported that she learned nothing, then both myself and the student needed to talk about why that was the case. Was it something on my part, or was it a lack of effort on hers? This was what both the student and myself needed to figure out so that we can either correct ourselves and make it better for the next time, or identify something as having worked well in order to repeat it. This reorientation is where the true learning takes place.

The Importance for Students

The logical question is, why have students reflect in the first place? They already have shown whether they have mastered the material or not. Why the additional step? What can it provide for students? The answer is: plenty. Self-reflection is a good teaching tool not just in the classroom, but in life in general. It is self-reflection which causes Lebron James—even after winning three NBA championships, as well as being nominated as MVP several times—to say to himself, "I need to work on my assists." After starting his amazing career with an average of six assists per game, in the last few years, that number has been around nine. It is the same tool used by Walt Disney to decide—after building a very successful animation studio that produced the likes of Snow White, Pinocchio, and Bambi—to bring the Disney magic to families on a daily basis by developing the idea for a theme park called Disneyland. He could have very well rested on the laurels of his earlier accomplishments, but thoughtful self-reflection led him to believe that he could accomplish even more. It is the strategy that you can use to become a better teacher. There is a reason you picked up this book; you have reflected upon your practice, and—like any teacher worth their salt—have determined that something can be better. I've often said that once you stop self-reflecting and think that you have this teaching thing down, it is time to retire, whether you are 3 or 30 years into your career.

The people who are the best in the world in the fields of sports, business, entertainment, and other endeavors get to be that way because they reflect upon their practices and understand there is always room for improvement. Why not teach this valuable skill to students at a very young age? What business wouldn't want an employee who realizes that she could be even better at her job? What wife wouldn't want a husband who can reflect upon his behavior and adapt over the years? There is real-world application to the art of self-reflection, so if we can get students in the habit of doing this, they will be better off for it.

One thing that reflection does is shifts the learning from the content to the student herself. It is no longer about *what* you learned, but *how* you learned it. It puts the students at the center of the learning process, which is consistent with what a culture of motivation tries to accomplish. There are other benefits for students, some of which include:

> **Recognition of mastery:** This is where the enduring understanding gets developed. By thinking about what was learned in class, whether it be content or a skill, students can identify any new knowledge that was gained

and how this leads to their growth. Too many students put the worth of their learning on the letter grade they receive. What really matters, though, is how much they grew and how much they allow this growth to stay with them.

Self-awareness: Not a lot of students are blessed with self-awareness. Heck, not a lot of adults possess it either. Being able to recognize a weaknesses or area for improvement is what leads to a student becoming better. If you can successfully compare what you learned with the tendencies you know about yourself, you can come to the conclusion of what you could have done better to get improved results.

Collaboration: Students often collaborate with others on work, so reflecting on how things went can be eye-opening. You might discover that as much as you like your best friend, they are not the best groupmate, or that student that doesn't seem to care about school actually has some pretty good ideas. If a student does not work well with a classmate, a thoughtful reflection might provide some insight into why this is, and maybe the student copes better with this person next time.

Thinking about the learning: There are many different types of learners. They have been described by Kolb's learning styles, Gardner's intelligences, and the very simple VAK, which stands for:

- Visual—learning best through imagery and seeing things;
- Auditory—learning best through listening and hearing things; and
- Kinesthetic—learning best through using one's hands and doing things.

Reflecting and figuring out what sort of learner you are and how you learn best is an immense advantage. This practice will help you in school and many other contexts. Exploring this by reflecting on what you learned best from the lesson and how this was delivered will help you to gain this understanding.

Dialogue: A reflection is a communication tool between student and teacher. The student puts something in her reflection about the way she learns. When the teacher reads this, she now understands the best way to get information across to the student. This communication should be a two-way street. Through either comments made about the reflection or conversations between the teacher and student, the teacher is providing feedback and possibly coaching how to handle a problem mentioned in the reflection. The reflection simply acts as another method with which you can have this dialogue.

As you can see, the benefits for students are many. This begs the question of whether you can afford to *not* use reflection in your classroom if you want students to get the most from their learning. There will be those who will argue that they do not have the time to do thoughtful reflection, but the reality is, if you move on to another lesson without reflecting, there is a good possibility that students will quickly forget what they learned, meaning that the time you spent with them was wasted. Reflection just ensures that this time is well spent.

The Importance for Teachers

As important as reflection is for the student, it is a great resource for the teacher as well. Although you are evaluated by your principal or supervisor, your true evaluators are your students. Getting valuable feedback from them as to what is working and what is not can improve your practice as a teacher. Our students have powerful voices, so listening to these as often as possible will make you a better teacher. I've been evaluated throughout my entire teaching career, and I maybe have gotten one or two pieces of good feedback that would change my practice. Students, however, have had a huge influence on how I adapt my teaching practices. Whether through reflection, surveys, conversations, or observable actions, I have refined, reshaped, and jettisoned lessons to make them better for the next group of students.

I learned the importance of student feedback while teaching for an academic summer camp the past decade. The way the camp is set up is ingenious. You propose a course to teach, writing up a description and basic outline of what will be accomplished, and they put it in the course manual. Students then sign up for courses—or, they don't. If your course doesn't sound very interesting, they will simply choose another one. If not enough students sign up for your course, they don't offer the class, and you don't get to teach it that summer. Your job and how many courses you get to teach relies solely on student feedback. Although students don't directly say to you, "I didn't pick your course because it doesn't sound that intriguing," they do say so with their actions. Luckily, I interested enough students that I had a full slate of classes, but then I ran into the second instance of feedback. At the end of the week-long class, students were asked to reflect. The format of this feedback was an anonymous survey that asked some probing questions about what they learned in the class, whether they would recommend this class to others, and what they would change, if anything. I found out very quickly—uh-oh!—students were telling me whether they liked the class or not and why this was. Was this something I wanted to hear? The answer, of course, was yes. This information was like gold to me. Because classes are taken based on interest, it was important to create a good word-of-mouth. Students could go to the camp for 3 years, so if someone liked my class, they might tell their roommate or kids who attend their school, and those students may sign up for my class the following year. If I wanted my classes to stay in business, I had to make sure that students were enjoying the class. As a result, my classes have morphed over the years due to student reflections and feedback that let me know what they thought worked, what they thought didn't work, how they would improve things, and/or what they really enjoyed. For example, I was teaching a class on historical mysteries, and I showed a video for one of the classes on Bigfoot, yet students shared that they thought the video was boring and perceived that this time would be better spent doing another activity. One student even suggested that we instead conduct a debate on whether Bigfoot existed or not. I thought this was an excellent idea, and have since canned the video and added the debate, which students have expressed that they like in their feedback.

Imagine how things would work in public schools if students could determine which courses were offered based upon interest, importance, and attainability. If their job depended on students signing up for their courses, teachers would get really good at adapting to their students' needs. We are often spoiled because the school fills our classrooms with students. But for other courses such as German, multimedia, and business, teachers must actively recruit students, and the best way to do that is to create a class that students would want to be in.

I carried this mindset over to my own classroom. I imagined how I would write up a description of the class that would make students want to take if they had a choice. Similarly, I began to use reflections in my class and use the responses as ways to make my class better. To this day, I use student reflection to mold my classes and programs of study. Student voice is really powerful to listen to, but you have to provide them with a forum to make this heard. That is what reflection does for teachers—it provides immediate, real-time feedback from your most important audience (your students), so that you can quickly adapt your class to make the learning better, relevant, and more meaningful for students.

The Use of Student Journaling

One method that I have used for reflection is to have students journal their thoughts. This method was useful this for a couple of reasons.

1. It was more stream-of-consciousness; thus, I was getting a good picture of their thought process and true insights.

2. It was less formal and more private, so students were willing to share information they may not have if they were put into a group situation.

I really didn't care about the format of the reflection. Students could write in a journal by hand, type in a Google Doc, or use FlipGrid to record their thoughts on video. Any method that could be shared with me was fair game. The only thing I asked was that students followed a basic structure, which looked like this:

Figure 8.1 *Reflection Cycle*

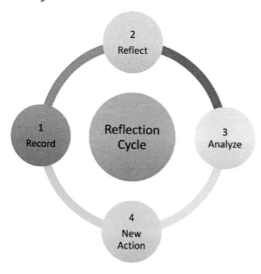

First, I wanted students just to report what went on, without any judgement or opinion. It was simply the facts. This caused them to pause for a moment and try to remember how things happened. This activated their recall, so they could provide their reflections in the second part. At this point, they stated their opinion of how things went, what they felt they learned, and whether there were any mistakes that they wished they could fix. It is in this section that you will gain a good idea of which of the goal valuations are important to your students. If a student complains that the assignment was just too difficult for him, attainability might be an important aspect of this motivation. If a student complains that she didn't see the purpose in doing the assignment in the first place, then focusing on importance might be a way to get her more motivated. This also might mean you need to be clearer in your visible learning so that she understands this importance.

Because reflection is not a normal practice in most classrooms, students will need some help at first in order to reflect effectively. I often used prompts to provide students with guidance. Once your class becomes more familiar with this strategy, the prompts may become less specific.

For example, if we are reflecting for the first time, my prompts might look like this:

> I want you to reflect upon the following from our visit to our class Native American Museum. Make sure you provide details and show us what you observed, not just tell.
>
> What is a single exhibit you thought was really good? What about the exhibit made it stand out from the others?
>
> Using a different exhibit than the one above, what was something you learned you hadn't known before that was interesting? What about this makes it interesting to you?
>
> Which of the geographic areas overall (i.e., Eastern Woodlands, Plains, Northwest Coast, Southwest) do you think did the best job of representing the culture? Why specifically do you feel this way? (Make sure to use examples of exhibits.)

What was something specifically you saw in some of the exhibits that you wished you would have used? Why would it have made your exhibit better?

You can see that these prompts are very content-specific. They direct students to consider what I would like them to think about, starting with the concrete examples of the exhibits, and eventually scaffolding up to the more abstract of how they could have made their own exhibit better. If it were later in the year, and students had more experience with reflections, I might ask something as simple as this:

What ideas from the exhibits you saw caused you to think about improvements to your own project?

If I put something like this at the beginning of the year, I'm more likely to not get many details, and the thoughts of the students will be surface-level. Once they have become used to the idea of a reflection, however, the need to guide them lessens, and I can simply ask them a simple prompt which they know they need to expound on.

Class/Group Discussions

You can also conduct reflections as a class or in small groups. This brings other voices into the conversation, and allows students to feed on and build upon one another's ideas. It also makes things more public, so it might be more challenging to get genuine responses from students. Because of this, it is very important to provide them with a safe space to share their thoughts and ideas with others without fear of judgment.

I've done these class discussions in a few ways. I mentioned one of these in a previous chapter when we had a disastrous project concerning Ancient Greece. We moved all of the desks out of the way and put the chairs in a giant circle. Then, we addressed the elephant in the room: Why did this project fail so badly? I got the discussion started, but for the most part, let students talk and either air their frustrations with the project or their disappointments with themselves.

If you are going to conduct a reflection with the entire class, my biggest piece of advice is to make sure you aren't doing most of the talking. I talked before about being a good listener, and this is the perfect opportunity for you to shut up and hear what your students have to say. It is not a time to be defensive or to explain your side of things. It is an opportunity to put everything out on the table—the good, the bad, and, often, the ugly—and figure out how to make it better for next time.

One thing you might do, especially if students are new to this process, is to develop discussion questions to guide student conversation. Students might not be confident to speak freely at first or be able to come up with an open-ended response that will elicit further conversation. Students are used to questions that they answer it to the best of their ability, and then the discussion is over. Your discussion questions should be designed to be open-ended so that students can not only share their thoughts and feelings, they can also bring up things that will cause other students to partake in the discussion or provide them with food for thought for their own reflections.

Here are some examples of open-ended reflection questions that may be used to spark a conversation:

- What class activities helped you learn the most? The least?
- What skills or strategies did you use to help you learn? Were there ones that might have been useful to have learned before working on this lesson?
- What help did you want from the teacher but didn't get? What were ways the teacher lent support and advanced your thinking?
- Is this what you expected or wanted your work to be?
- What did you do to help your learning? What did you do to hurt your learning?
- If you had a time machine and could go back to the beginning of this lesson, what advice would you give yourself that

could improve your performance?

- The next time you get to do this activity or one similar to it, what mistakes will you avoid and what successes will you repeat?

- Why might learning this skill/content be important now? One year from now? Ten years from now?

- What is the most important thing you learned during this lesson, either good or bad?

- What can you do now that you were not able to do last week/month/quarter/year?

- Do you think you truly demonstrated how you mastered this learning objective?

You can also do these reflections in small groups. Break the students either randomly or purposefully into groups, and ask these same questions, allowing them to discuss as a group. The challenge of doing this is that you cannot possibly lead the discussion for five or six groups, so they will have to ask the questions and drive the conversations; however, this can be a good thing. You can help them by putting the questions you want them to consider on index cards and putting them in the center of the group, but you also must be willing to allow them to take the conversation where it goes, even if it seems as though it has gone entirely off the tracks.

You could also have the students generate the reflection questions. Have them take a few minutes to jot down some questions they believe need to be answered concerning this lesson. Then, use these as fuel for the discussion.

If students worked together in a group, you might give them the opportunity to reflect on the success of the collaboration, or whether there were things they could have done to improve the synergy of the group. It is important that you develop norms that prevent this from turning into a finger-pointing exercise with students blaming one another. At the same time, if two students had a conflict while working together, they should be given the space to work this out in a controlled and constructive manner. Hearing from others will provide students with a chance to see what they look like to others. The student might have perceived that he was helpful to the group, while multiple group members might have just seen this as bossiness. This is part of developing awareness and what you do and do not bring to a group.

What I would sometimes do with students was to hand them back their group grade in the form of a rubric with lots of feedback on it. Then, I would tell them to imagine this grade as a pie. Did they think that each member of the group deserved an equal piece of the pie, or did some contribute to the group mightily while others brought the group down? If the group received a B- overall, the group may determine that Student 1 actually deserves an A- for the part she played, while Student 2 might have deserved a C because he often distracted the group or did not do his part. Some groups would merely decide that everyone deserved this grade equally, but I wanted to provide them with the space to have this conversation. Again, norms need to be put in place so that it does not devolve into an argument, but instead is a true reflection of what group members brought to the overall success and/or failure of the lesson.

Another way to set this up is to have students reflect with partners. Because you have a shared experience, it gives you someone to bounce ideas off of and to learn their perspective of how the lesson went. Your partner might also ask you questions you might not ask of yourself, deepening the reflection. In order for these types of reflections to work, boundaries for where the conversation goes might need to be established by laying down norms. Some of these norms might be:

- Keep the conversation positive, even when being critical.
- What is said between partners stays between partners.

- Make sure your feedback is designed to be productive.
- Ask questions designed to challenge thinking.
- Be honest, but do so with respect.
- Don't complain about something without an alternative solution.
- Use forward thinking (i.e., how will you use this information down the road).

A final way to have a reflection is an individual conference with a student. I like these because in addition to being a good way to help students to reflect upon best practices and possible improvements, it allows me to get to know them better. It is part of the caring aspect of the culture of motivation. If students see you sitting down with them and helping them to try and do better, they will feel cared for. This individual conference also ensures that students clearly understand the feedback that you give them. If you simply handed them back a graded piece of work with extensive comments, they could easily dismiss this and just look at the grade. If you are instead having a conversation about this feedback, you can be sure that they are hearing it and will hopefully use it to improve in the future.

If you are going to reflect in this manner, you have to be willing to be just as vulnerable as you expect students to be. Let's say you make a comment about something she did not include in her paper you graded, but she is able to show you where it is and that you just overlooked it, you have to eat your crow and admit you have made a mistake. Some teachers think this shows a lack of authority, but what it does is humanize and makes you more approachable. This reflection is a two-way street, and you need to be reflective of your own practices as a teacher if you expect students to do the same.

The Use of Protocols

At times, I would use protocols with students in order to aim their reflection in a productive direction. There are many protocols that can be accessed at the School Reform Initiative. I shared the snapshot protocol in Chapter Two, and will share three of my favorites.

A really basic protocol is known as the Driscoll Model of Reflection. It is broken down into three parts; the *what, so what,* and *now what.* In the "what" you are just asking for facts from the lesson:

What?

- descriptive

- facts, what happened, with whom

- substance of group interaction

You give students a few minutes to either jot some of these facts down or to discuss them with other students. This is basically just a recall of the events that took place during the lesson. It is important not to bring opinions or judgment into this part of motivation. This will happen in the "now what" phase of the protocol:

So what?

- meaning of experience for each participant

- feelings involved, lessons learned

- why?

Here, a shift occurs from just the descriptive to the interpretive. What did students think of certain things? Why did they think things went a certain way? What lessons were learned? At this point, we are scaffolding up to the student expressing her feelings about the lesson. We started with just what happened, and now that she has remembered this, she explains the why of the lesson. This is not the why you were looking for as the teacher, but the why that she got. You might spend more than a few minutes on this section, asking students to take the list of facts from the first part and reflecting how they felt about each of these.

This takes us to the final stage of the Driscoll Reflection: the "now what." In other words, what do we do to move forward concerning this lesson?

Now what?

- contextual—seeing this situation's place in the big picture
- applying lessons learned/insights gained to new situations
- setting future goals, creating an action plan

The main goal of this part of the reflection is to help students to see the context of the lesson. How will they use this skill or information in the future? Where might they see it cropping up in their own lives, and how will they handle that? What are lessons learned from the failures the student made? During this time, you want to see students making connections between the classroom and their lives. This is an additional scaffold and brings it back to the student, helping them to see the relevance and as a result, the importance.

This protocol structure can be done in groups, individually, in written form, or through dialogue; the possibilities are many, which is why I like it so much. I also like it because it starts students out easy and then takes the reflection much deeper. Some students have trouble getting below the surface. This protocol helps them to dig a little deeper and hopefully come to the realization of "this is why I learned this."

A protocol that I like to use for a quick reaction or feedback from students is the fortune cookie protocol. The parameters are fairly simple:

- If you could sum all of your takeaways from this lesson into a single sentence, what would it be?
- Try to phrase it like a fortune cookie, where there is a lesson to be learned or something to think about.
- Examples:
  - Big journeys begin with a single step
  - He who waits to the last minute usually gets left behind
  - Learn public speaking now, reap the benefits later

- I learned to multiply fractions

I like this one for a couple of reasons. It forces students to boil down what they learned into a single sentence. It acts as an exit ticket, showing the teacher what students got from it. It also shows me what was important to them. If 20 students in my classroom put statements about frustration, then I know that this is an issue I need to address. If some students seem to be missing the mark, I can have conversations with them to get them back on track. It is also fun to see the clever phrases students come up with. While some take a very straightforward approach and just put what they learned, others embrace the creativity of phrasing it like a fortune cookie.

To make it more authentic, I give each student a sticky note and have them write their phrase on it. When they leave the classroom, they place it on one of my bulletin boards or white boards near the door. Collectively, these sticky notes tell a story of how well the lesson went. Sometimes I will leave them there, and we reflect on them as a class later, or I might write some feedback or encouragements which the student can read the following day.

The final example is appropriately called the final word protocol. This is a good protocol to use when reflecting in groups. The way it works is as follows. Five or so students sit in a circle. The first person shares something they learned or something that was insightful for them. This is done in a sentence or so, and is given as a statement without judgment or opinion. Going around the circle, each student has 1 minute to comment on what was shared. You will need a timekeeper who lets others know when their minute is up, or the teacher can be the one who monitors this for all groups. If the student doesn't use the entire minute, the clock keeps ticking and the group merely reflects in silence. The comments students make might be an agreement, a feeling they had, something they would like to expand further on, or any commentary on what the initial student shared. It finally comes back to the original person who explains why he picked what he did, whether he agreed with what people said, or any other thing he would like to share about it, giving him the final word.

This is a good group activity for a few reasons. First is the obvious one of everyone getting the chance to voice their opinions. There are students who tend to dominate a discussion, while others dissolve into the background. This way, everyone gets the same opportunity to share their thoughts. Second, it forces students to have to listen. In some discussions, everyone is talking, but no one is listening, so an insightful comment or important message gets lost through bad listening. A third reason is that it keeps students focused, because they really don't have the time to get sidetracked or digress about something. Only having 1 minute to speak forces them to choose their words carefully and to stay on topic.

The important thing about protocols is that to match the protocol with the sort of reflection you wish to see from students. If you are just looking to determine mastery, a protocol that allows them to do this would be appropriate. If instead you are wanting students to self-reflect and gain awareness of the type of learner they are, you will need a protocol that gives them the guidance and space to explore this. You will find protocols that you like more than others. I do try and mix them up so that students are not reflecting the same way every time.

Finding the Heart of It

It is essential to have reflection in your class because this is where the endurance of learning takes root. Without thoughtful reflection, valuable lessons might be lost that would benefit students down the road and even in their lives. In order for it to work successfully, you have to establish a culture of thoughtful reflection. If you simply tack it onto the end of a lesson, rather than making it a part of your classroom practice, then it will not be as powerful for students. This will allow students to see the value of it and be motivated to use it. This will allow them to become better learners.

For further explanation, watch a video tutorial at
https://youtu.be/BCPtFaXSeZM.

HOW THE HELL DO WE MOTIVATE THESE KIDS?

Conclusion

DR. SEUSS, OR, HOW I LEARNED TO STOP WORRYING ABOUT THE TEST

"Miss Bonkers rose, 'Don't fret,' she said.
'You've learned the things you need
To pass that test and many more—
I'm certain you'll succeed.
We've taught you that the earth is round.
That red and white make pink.
And something else that matters more—
We've taught you how to think.'"
- Dr. Seuss

D r. Seuss has written many classic children's books filled with infinite wisdom for kids and adults alike. Who can forget how he taught us prejudice using the Sneetches and the stars on their bellies, or how the Lorax fought for the trees before it was the trendy thing to do? I'm sure that kids just heard a funny story about an elephant sitting on an egg, but moms and dads knew that Horton's story was about parental rights and who was more deserving of custody.

Yes, Dr. Seuss left us many wonderful tales that we continue to read to our children to this day. One of his unfinished works is entitled *Hooray for Diffendoofer Day*. It is the story of a school in Dinkerville where teachers teach in a manner that is non-traditional. For example:

Miss Bobble teaches listening,

Miss Wobble teaches smelling.

Miss Fribble teaches laughing,

And Miss Quibble teaches yelling. (Seuss, 1998, p. 2)

This is in stark contrast to the teachers in nearby Flobbertown. The kids worry about being sent to Flobbertown because "everyone in Flobbertown does everything the same." They continue:

It's miserable in Flobbertown,

They dress in just one style.

They sing one song, they never dance,

They march in single file. (Seuss, 1998, p. 22)

Now, I don't know about you, but Flobbertown sounds like a lot of schools I know of where everything is done the same way in the interest of compliance. This system stands in contrast to that of Dinkerville, where they all teach differently and get the kids excited about learning.

Like most teachers, I used to worry about the year-end test. I was afraid that I wouldn't have enough time to cover the required content standards and ensure that students could master—and remember— the material by the time March rolled around. I would do all sorts of test prep to ensure that students were ready—at least long enough to take the state test. My results were always pretty good, so it seemed as though my strategies were working.

After my first few years of uninspired teaching, feeling as though I was beating my head against the wall trying to get seventh and eighth graders to remember content that we spent weeks on, I took inspiration from the teachers in the Dinkerville school:

It looks like any other school,

But we suspect it's not.

I think we're learning lots of things

Not taught at other schools.

Our teachers are remarkable,

They make up their own rules. (Seuss, 1998, p. 1)

I started to make up my own rules. I started using project-based learning more and more in my classroom. No one else was doing this at my school. I was not implored by administration to do this; I just saw that it worked well with kids. When students of mine would visit me from the high school, they never once mentioned that they remembered doing a worksheet, or a passage in the textbook, or a multiple-choice test they took. They always remembered the projects we did. I thought to myself, "If this is what they are remembering, why not give them more of it?"

That is just what I did. I transformed my classroom into a project-based learning classroom, working in some problem- and case-based material as well; pretty soon, we were no longer using the textbook upon which I had previously relied so heavily. We were no longer taking the unit tests created in the same format as the state test, and I no longer did the test prep that monopolized the month leading up to the test. And guess what? My students did *better* on the state test. I concluded that in the long run, the content we are forcing students to know isn't as relevant as the motivation they are using to learn it.

I am not suggesting that you teach whatever you want to and hope for the best when the test comes. What I am saying is that there is a way to teach the content standards our subject area and grade level requires of us, while at the same time using strategies that teach children how to learn. In such an environment, they will enjoy going to school because school is the place where they get to learn about things that are relevant to their life. This is when their love of learning will return.

HOW THE HELL DO WE MOTIVATE THESE KIDS?

References

Ainsworth, L., & Donovan, L. (2019). *Rigorous curriculum design* (2nd ed.). International Center for Leadership in Education.

Almarode, J. T., & Vandas, K. L. (2018). *Clarity for learning: Five essential practices that empower teachers and students.* Corwin Press.

Anderman, E. M., & Murdock, T. B. (Eds.). (2007). *Psychology of academic cheating.* Elsevier Academic Press.

Black, P., & William, D. (2009). Developing the theory of formative assessment. *Educational Assessment, Evaluation and Accountability, 21*(1), 5–31.

Busteed, B. (2013, January 7). The school cliff: Student engagement drops with each school year. *Gallup Blog.* https://news.gallup.com/opinion/gallup/170525/school-cliff-student-engagement-drops-school-year.aspx

The Center for Comprehensive School Reform and Improvement. (2008). *Issue brief: Gifted and talented students at risk for underachievement.* Learning Point Associates and SEDL for the U.S. Department of Education.

Chazelle, D. (2014). *Whiplash.* Blumhouse Productions.

Conagra Brands. (2020, June 17). *Conagra Brands announces Mrs. Butterworth's brand review.* https://www.conagrabrands.com/

news-room/news-conagra-brands-announces-mrs-butter-worths-brand-review-prn-122733

Gould, S., & Weller, C. (2015, October 1). The most common reasons students drop out of high school are heartbreaking. *Business Insider.* https://www.businessinsider.com/most-common-reasons-students-drop-out-of-high-school-2015-10.

Hattie, J. (2009). *Visible learning: A synthesis of over 800 meta-analyses relating to achievement.* Routledge.

Jetter, R., & Coda, R. (2018). *Let them speak: How student voice can transform your school.* Dave Burgess Consulting.

Kage, M. (1991). *The effects of evaluation on intrinsic motivation.* Paper presented at the meeting of the Japan Association of Educational Psychology, Joetsu, Japan.

Kohn, A. (2018). *Punished by rewards: The trouble with gold stars, incentive plans, A's, praise, and other bribes.* Mariner Books.

Lahey, J. (2016). *The gift of failure: How the best parents learn to let go so their children can succeed.* Harper.

Llopis, G. (2013, May 20). 6 ways effective listening can make you a better leader. *Forbes.* https://www.forbes.com/sites/glennllopis/2013/05/20/6-effective-ways-listening-can-make-you-a-better-leader/?sh=62d431511756

Ludema, J., & Johnson, A. (2018, April 15). Five questions you can ask instead of 'how are you?' *Forbes.* https://www.forbes.com/sites/amberjohnson-jimludema/2018/04/05/five-questions-you-can-ask-instead-of-how-are-you/

Mackenzie, T. (2017). *Dive into inquiry: Amplify learning and empower student voice.* EdTechTeam Press.

Marzano, R. J., Pickering, D. J., & Pollock, J. E. (2001). *Classroom instruction that works: Research-based strategies for increasing student achievement.* Association for Supervision and Curriculum Development.

Nottingham, J. (2013). *Encouraging learning: How you can help children learn.* Routledge.

Patall, E. A., Cooper, H., & Robinson, J. C. (2008). The effects of choice on intrinsic motivation and related outcomes: A meta-analysis of research findings. *Psychological Bulletin, 134,* 270-300.

Pulfrey, C., Buch, C., & Butera, F. (2011). Why grades engender performance-avoidance goals: The mediating role of autonomous motivation. *Journal of Educational Psychology, 103,* 683-700.

Quinn, F. M. (2000). Reflection and reflective practice. In C. Davies, L. Finlay, & A. Bullman (Eds.), *Changing practice in health and social care.* SAGE.

Seuss, Dr., Prelutsky, J., & Smith, L. (1998). *Hooray for Diffendoofer Day.* Knopf Books for Young Readers.

Shute, V. J. (2008). Focus on formative feedback. *Review of Educational Research, 78*(1), 153–189.

Stanley, T. (2014). *Performance-based assessment for 21st century learning.* Prufrock Press.

Titsworth, S., Mazer, J. P., Goodboy, A. K., Bolkan, S., & Myers, S. A. (2015). Two meta-analyses exploring the relationship between teacher clarity and student learning. *Communication Education, 64*(4), 385-418.

Vislon, J. (2014). *This is not a test: A new narrative on race, class, and education.* Haymarket Books.

Willingham, D. (2009). *Why don't students like school?* Jossey-Bass.

Wolpert-Gawron, H. (2018). *Just ask us: Kids speak out on student engagement.* Corwin Press.

Worthington, R. E. (2014). *Corporate Recruiters Survey: 2014 survey report.* Graduate Management Admission Council.